Invited.

Invited.

A Celebration of Spiritual Direction

Diane Carver Mann

Larry Warner

RESOURCE *Publications* · Eugene, Oregon

INVITED.
A Celebration of Spiritual Direction

Resource Publications
An Imprint of Wipf and Stock Publishers
199 W. 8th Ave., Suite 3
Eugene, OR 97401

www.wipfandstock.com

PAPERBACK ISBN: 978-1-5326-1695-2
HARDCOVER ISBN: 978-1-4982-4103-8
EBOOK ISBN: 978-1-4982-4102-1

Manufactured in the U.S.A.

This book is dedicated to Barbara Carver Franzen,
for noticing the grace—and inviting me to notice it too.

Contents

CONTENTS

Foreword

I have had the privilege of journeying with Diane, formally and informally, for over eight years. I can remember interviewing her as she sought to discern whether to enroll in a two-year course in spiritual formation and spiritual direction I was directing at the time. I remember her desire to go deeper with God, her excitement around learning and growing in Christ, and her own doubts about being up for the task. After spending time with her, it did indeed feel like this was the right time and program for her. She agreed and began a journey that she faithfully continues to walk to this day—a journey of being and becoming the person God has created her, called her, and is empowering her to be—and companioning with others to do the same.

I have watched over the years as she has continued to be more and more comfortable in her own skin—willing to own her voice, to write, and to sing her songs, even sharing her own songs and poetry with others. Now she has written this book. She has been and remains an inspiration to me, and I hope this book is not her last. As you read her words in the following pages, you will begin to see and appreciate her authenticity, desire to grow, and willingness to be honest with herself, with God, and with her spiritual director. You will see the unique ways that she views life, learns from God, and interacts with God through the raw materials of her everyday life. You will notice her interactions with others and her awareness of the stirrings in her own heart.

However, this book is only partly about Diane. In many ways it is a tribute to the precious companion God gave Diane to help her be and become the person God created her to be. The words of her spiritual director-soul-friend-aunt comprise much of this book. The collection of sayings from her spiritual director—words of wisdom, insight, and encouragement—helped Diane see, discover, reflect on (and partner with) what God has done in and through her during their years of journeying together.

As you make your way through this book. I invite you to pay special attention to the words Diane writes at the beginning of each chapter. I believe these words will speak deeply to your own story, your personal journey, and serve to encourage you along the path. Diane makes it quite clear that we are healed and yet broken and it is God's love, grace, and forgiveness, and our willingness to be dependent upon God that makes living this life possible. And, of course, it does not hurt to have a life-tested, Jesus-loving, wise spiritual companion to help one along the journey of opening oneself to God in ways that bring life, love, hope, and encouragement to continue the voyage.

Larry Warner

Author
Journey with Jesus
Discernment, God's Will & Living Jesus

Preface

"Thank you for coming to my house!" I am known to say to visitors. My children often quote me saying this, and my grown nieces and nephews still remember my excited greeting from their earliest visits. I said it upon their arrival, and I said it upon their departure. I consider it a gift that someone would invest their time visiting with me. So to you, reader, I say now, with my whole heart, thank you for coming to my book!

Each chapter opens with a reflection by me, where I share some of my story and what I am learning. These reflections contain what I am noticing on my sometimes bumpy but adventurous journey. I then provide collections of sayings, wise words from my spiritual director she wrote as she listened to my heart through our years of journeying together. These are words I have carried with me, chewed on, and digested, words leading me to relate with God, just as I am—words I trust will bless you and help you step more into the reality of God's love and longing for you, just as you are.

You will notice at the end of each chapter absolutely no questions. The most helpful questions I have ever been asked while reading any written material are these:

"What does this lead you to want to pray?" and "To what might God be inviting you?" I invite you to keep these questions in mind as you read.

The book can be read through quickly, but I would encourage you to travel through it slowly, noticing your internal reactions to what you're reading. For example, if you come upon a delightful reminder of the truth of who God is or who you are because of him, sit with it, savor it. If a topic is difficult for you, notice it, hold it before God, wrestle with God, if necessary—express to God your reactions.

My spiritual director, Aunt Barb, always opens our e-mail direction sessions with a prayer asking God to lead our time together. I share below one of the prayers she has prayed for me, and I pray this for you, dear reader. Again, thank you for coming to my book!

> Lord Jesus, thank you for inviting us into your presence. Thank you that all of our lives are rooted in, surrounded by, and tended to by you, and because of that, we are free to be and become the people you have called us to be. Help us now to pay attention to you, to give ourselves to you to the extent that we are able, that you might do in and through us that which brings glory to you as we explore what you have for us in this place.
>
> Amen

Acknowledgments

While on a personal writing retreat at a friend's timeshare, I floated in the lazy river. Palm trees swayed above, waving their branches like encouraging spectators. As I lay looking up at them, one by one I gave thanks to God for the many people who have cheered me on while writing this book. Paula, Jeanne, Diane, Sheryl, Debbie, and Tammi, all read my early chapters when the idea for this book was in the embryonic stage. They offered friendship, feedback, prayers, and words that put courage into me. I can't count how many times they've listened to me say, "My Aunt Barb says," (fill in the blank). Thanks to Chris for lending me her timeshare! Her generosity gave me space to focus on writing.

I am grateful for the prayers and excitement from my cousins Debbie and Connie and for Mardelle, who dropped by with coffee when I was immersed in writing and sent rah-rah texts. Larry was helpful by sometimes writing to me asking, "How's the book coming?" It made me work writing into my schedule in order to give an honest answer, and his question made the book seem like a real thing. Lynn listened to me, cheered me on, and reminded me often about those small but essential baby steps. Elizabeth, wow. She helped me over hurdles that would have stopped me in my tracks. Well, sometimes they did stop me, but she patiently helped me work through them, and I learned much about myself and the creative process along the way. She offered daily emoji accountability towards the end of the project and believed in me and this from the beginning.

Andrew, my son-in-law, who was visiting from Texas when I was daunted by the final steps for manuscript submission, stepped in with his formatting and editing skills and all he knows about books and basically saved the day, navigating me through unchartered waters. What a surprise gift he brought. My womb-to-the-tomb friend, Trish, with her persistence and love for life, inspires much of who I am and what I do. I'll never stop learning from, being shaped by, and giving thanks for my four unmerited gifts from God—Ryan, Kyle, Karis, and Megan.

To Brent, my husband, my co-adventurer, my friend, and my navigator, you are the best listener I know. Talking to you about what I am learning and what God is up to gives me clarity. I know our talks make your rocket scientist brain have to jump over to the other hemisphere, and I appreciate it. I would be lost without you (you know it's true!).

Finally, Aunt Barbara, what can I say? I smile when I think of what God has done through our spiritual direction relationship. He knew way before we did what he had in mind for us. I think he smiles too. I did not know how to thank you for your investing your time, wisdom, and love in me. I could have sent a thank-you card, I suppose, but instead I wrote this book.

Diane Mann

July, 2017
Chino, California

Introduction

Invited to Spiritual Direction

M y father died on January 7, 2000, nineteen months after falling from a roof. He severed his spinal cord, becoming paralyzed from the neck down and ventilator dependent. In the months following his accident, while I assisted with his care at my parents' home, some of his sisters visited. I was excited to meet some aunts from my father's side for the very first time, but I made no significant connections with any of them during their visit. Their short stay was spent reconnecting with each other and their newly injured brother. The following year, when my husband planned a winter trip to the East Coast for me and our four children, I arranged to visit my Aunt Barbara, the youngest sister of my father's, in Pittsburgh.

Our family spent no more than an hour and a half in her home laughing, sharing some snacks, and getting to know one another. My aunt looks like my dad, has many of his mannerisms, including a tremendous wit and kindness akin to his. She was raised by my grandpa, whom I met only once, and my grandma Carver, who died the year I was born. Grandma was a woman about whom I had always been curious, having only heard lovely things about her. Needless to say, I was eager to get to know my aunt! We sat at their table munching goodies. As she talked, I hung on to each word she said. I couldn't hide the joy I felt during our visit. Wisdom oozed from her, and I absorbed each word she spoke.

She and I stood in her kitchen while she heated some tomato soup on the stove. She was showing me something in the Bible, and we were deep in talk and thought. The soup boiled over, but she hardly noticed because she was engrossed in our conversation. This is something I would have done, and it reminded me of me!

"Mom," my kids whispered to me on the walk out of Aunt Barb's home, "I thought she was going to call us turkeys, just like Grandpa used to!" They too noticed her resemblance to their grandpa. As we drove away, I noticed in our van a small notebook I purchased on the trip. It was beautiful. Covered with red and white flowers, three inches by four inches, its beauty had called to me from a store display. I had bought it without a purpose in mind. My heart leapt as I got the idea to write questions about God and life in the notebook then mail it to Aunt Barb across the country. I thought she could respond then send the notebook back to me and we could engage in a back-and-forth conversation. The desire to be in some kind of a mentoring relationship with her was planted in me at that moment.

I introduced my idea to her a couple years later when she called me to arrange for her daughter to stay with us a few days in California. "You know what will happen," she said, "with how absentminded we both can be, one of us will probably receive the notebook in the mail then lose it and not mail it back. And I'm afraid it will be me!" She didn't think we would be very success-ful with such an arrangement. I agreed, and we both laughed and dismissed the idea.

I had experienced severe depression following my father's death in 2000. Five years' experimentation with different antide-pressants, which proved ineffective, had been discouraging. In 2002 I was diagnosed with hepatitis C, which I acquired in 1976 through a blood transfusion following spinal surgery when I was thirteen years old. In 2003 I received a year's protocol of chemo-therapy-type treatment to fight the hepatitis C virus. At the con-clusion of treatment, all tests indicated I was cured, but I suffered from post-treatment depression and entered a dark time emotion-ally. The darkness became much deeper when, six months later, I learned the virus had returned. The walls of the examining room closed in on me as an intern reported, "Don't worry. You won't have cirrhosis of the liver for five more years." I was in a physical crisis, an emotional crisis, and a spiritual crisis.

In 2005, a Carver cousin arranged a family reunion in Wyoming. My sister Susan and I traveled together, and there was no shortage of excitement between us. We arrived early to a lodge where the reunion was to take place. Shortly after we arrived, Aunt Barb and her husband showed up. We had a fantastic time meeting never-before-known-to-us cousins, and our Aunt Barb and Uncle Jim took us under their wings and poured love into us during the weekend.

The last morning of our weekend reunion in Wyoming, I was at breakfast with my relatives when Aunt Barb turned to me and asked in her kind, compassionate way, "Are you taking care of you?" She saw right into my soul, it seemed, and I couldn't come up with a fake answer. Neither could I keep shut the gate holding back my tears, so together the tears and my honest feelings flowed. I told her some of how I had been suffering and suffered still. I told her how very shaken I was, and how spiritually disoriented I had become. She listened with understanding. She listened with compassion and empathy. She listened without judgment. I felt pretty sure that if God had ears, they were a lot like hers. Physically she looked so much like my earthly father had looked, but her presence emanated the heart of my heavenly Father.

When Susan and I left the lodge, we said to Aunt Barb and Uncle Jim, "Thank you for loving us!" to which they replied, "What's not to love?" What joy it brought us to spend time with them.

Two months later I received a note in the mail from Aunt Barb. This is what it said:

Dear Diane,

I have thought of you so often since our wonderful time with you and Susan at the reunion. Please say "hi" and give her a big hug for me. I'm not the greatest correspondent, as you may have guessed, but you have been on my heart. I don't know whether you have sought out your little

*old lady spiritual mentor, but if that is not a possibility I
would be willing to try out an e-mail relationship with you
that perhaps God would use to help you over some of the
"bumps." I'm not sure exactly what this would look like,
"spiritual direction" via e-mail, but if you think it would
be helpful, I would try to work out the logistics. It would
definitely be preferable if you could find someone there,
but maybe something is better than nothing. Let me know
what you think. Maybe Susan could set you up with an
e-mail account on her computer.*

    I hope you can read this. My handwriting is atrocious.

Love and prayers,

    Barb

She received certification as a spiritual director in 2004 from
Sursum Corda Spiritual Directors Formation Program and began offering spiritual direction to others. In 2005 we began our
spiritual direction relationship. As I write this book, we have met
via week-long e-mail discussions over 110 times, contacting each
other the second Monday of each month. Our sessions last a few
days. She opens by sending a prayer. I pray the prayer with her
then share what is going on in my life. She asks questions. She
encourages me to ask God questions, to wait for him, look for him,
to thank him, to tell him all I have told her. Together we wait for
God and seek to sense God's heartbeat in my life. As she listens
prayerfully, here and there she gives insights and bits of wisdom as
God's spirit leads her.

I often share these wise words of hers with others, cutting
and pasting from our communications, sending them in e-mails
and texts or bringing up things she has said in conversations. It
is these insights I share in this book: the words she has spoken to
nudge me toward exploring and relating with God. If I were to
print up all our conversations, I would have a several-foot-high
stack of pages.

I look at the little notebook I had desired to fill, and I look
at what God had for me instead. I have a hard time taking it
in. My heart bulges with gratitude for God's inviting me to this

spiritual direction relationship, for what he has shown me of himself through my aunt, and for the ways God has drawn me into a more intimate place of relating with him.

God is described in Ephesians 3:20 as "him who is able to do far more abundantly than all we ask or think." He has been lavish in satisfying my longings to know him more and my desire to have someone journey with me spiritually. My dreams look tiny when I compare them with what God has brought about.

I have titled this book "Invited" to celebrate my invitation to spiritual direction and God's invitation to meet me in new ways. I write it with pouring-out gratitude to God. I write it to honor and thank my Aunt Barb, celebrating what God has shown us on this journey. And I write it to share with you some of her words, words inviting us all to splash in the bigger-than-we-know love of Jesus.

1

Invited to Love

Freedom from Fear

A good friend made the where-to-start-this-book quandary easier for me by asking, "What does God's love feel like to you?" Her inquiry sent me back to memories of the earliest sessions with my spiritual director. I wasn't sensing God's love in my life, longed to know the love God has for me, and found myself striving to receive it rather than resting in its reality. Anxiety pinned me to my bed. I would leave my fitful place of rest only to do what was required in caring for my family. I begged God to calm my heart, but the fierce storm continued. I quoted scripture, sang songs, pleaded for relief from angst and pain in my hurting soul, for paralyzing fear to go away. Accompanying these powerful feelings of fear was a magnification of negative ways I saw myself. I had struggled with an underlying sense I was not quite enough and felt deformed, invisible, and plain.

My director would tell me of God's love, as would my friends and teachers. I filled in the blanks of my Bible study lessons with diligence. I wrote down God's declarations of love on paper but desperately needed God to write his love onto the blanks of my heart. My director urged me to find a spot in my home wherein I would meet God daily. Beginning with five minutes at a time, she encouraged me to quiet my thoughts and allow God access to my heart and sit in his love. "I don't do anything regularly," I informed her. "I don't do anything consistently," vehemently resisting God's invitation to let him love me.

There were days where the four feet from my bed to the couch in my bedroom, which I had chosen as my meeting place with God, seemed an ocean's distance. Most days I swam the miles, sometimes crawling on my knees from bed to couch. I sat. I waited. I felt foolish. "If you really loved me, why would I have to sit here and pretend like you love me?" I silently prayed. Yet I found myself returning to my couch if I was hurting later in the day or I felt stressed, just to sit in the love of God. Mostly there was no sensation of love in those very moments—just quiet, just me, just God in me and I in God. I gave God access to my heart and asked him to take me, surrendered just as I was, and to help me lean not on what was in my head but to trust him in my heart.

Barb suggested that I end each day asking God, "Where were places in my day wherein you were loving me and I noticed? Wherein were places you were trying to capture my attention with your love and I didn't notice?" Gradually I began to recognize God's love. I began to live as one who is loved.

I do not know when the tune began—perhaps he was singing it to me all along—but finally God's song of love quieted me, and I was in a place to receive love.

Recognizing and receiving God's love is a lifelong (and beyond) journey. In answer to the question with which this chapter began, feeling God's love is living with my head lifted high because Christ's hand is holding up my chin. God's love grants a confidence to run to the maker of the universe even when I have failed yet again. It is a merciful look at myself and others, sensing God's patience with me, sometimes even his delight in me, his protection of me, his reception of me, and his longing for me. It is noticing God's invitations to me to be with him in brand-new ways. Sometimes I feel God's love in a spin on the beach or a hug from a friend. It is living in his tender gaze that rests upon me. It is loving him back!

Here are some words from Aunt Barb inviting me to God's love:

My guess is that the biggest stumbling block in all of our lives
is the failure to know how much God loves us.

∾

The Lord loves us unconditionally, no matter what we
manage to mess up, confuse, or damage.

∾

It is always a good thing to wallow in the love of God.

∾

When we are viewed through eyes of love, we are amazingly
set free. As we love others, they too are set free.

∾

Allow Jesus to love you in the midst of your fear.

∾

It is good to acknowledge fear before the Lord
and have a conversation about it.

∾

The more we experience the love of God, the less we
find ourselves needing to fear.

∾

As we hang out with Jesus, allowing him to love us, that love
flows in and through us to others. It just does.

∾

The only remedy I know for fear is the love
which Jesus has for us.

∾

The psalmist says, "When I am afraid, I will put my trust in
Thee" (Ps 56:3). He can do this because of his knowledge of
the protective love of God.

∾

The more we live out of the ocean of God's love for us, the more free we are to be what he had in mind for us to be from the beginning. Love sets us free in ways nothing else can.

∼

It is always good to remind ourselves of the love of God. He loves us because he loves us because he loves us—sick or healthy, weak or strong, rebellious or obedient. That love extends to those around us as well.

∼

We are definitely complex creatures. God is merciful, loving, kind and transforming.

∼

Take some time to reflect sitting at the foot of the cross, soaking in some of that *encompassing* love, realizing how much you are worth, allowing Christ to make that love personal, real, and accessible.

∼

Nothing can separate you from Christ's love. This is a truth that seems to triumph over all the others.

∼

Behold him, and allow him to hold you.

∼

He is always with us despite our appearance, our lack of physical ability, our ability to look good or even to think well.

∼

The Lord Jesus knows your heart, keeps loving you anyway, and keeps pressing you back on himself.

∼

Love is really all there is to the gospel. It's God's love that saves us, sustains us, and compels us. It is the love of God that sets us free, and his love working in and through us enables us to set each other free. How good is the love of God!

～

Remember that you are one whom the Lord rejoices over with singing. He rejoices over your loved ones as well. All of us are precious in the sight of God.

～

The truth is that we are enveloped in the love of God.

～

Isn't it good that your heavenly Father wants the same thing that you do?! Your longing for God of course stems from his deep longing for you. We do love him because he first loved us. These deep longings are his gift that he wants you to more and more unwrap.

～

Remember to ask the Lord what he loves. You will find that you are at the center of that huge, loving embrace.

～

We are complex creatures and fallen creatures. And although we are redeemed, our motives are not always pure. Fortunately, God loves us anyway.

～

God is always speaking words of love, often through the words of scripture, which then become alive in us as living bread.

～

God really wants you to know that he loves you! Ask him to open your eyes to see, and then actually verbalize that love, either aloud or to yourself, "Thank you, Lord, for loving me by _____."

～

Bottom line: God loves you because he loves you
because he loves you.

⌒

The Lord Jesus knows about your fear. He does not condemn
you about it. He merely wants you to come to him
and allow his perfect love to cast it out.

⌒

Fortunately, God does not think that, if we were different, he
would be more loving. That little thought just popped into my
head, to focus not on you but on God's so very unconditional
love toward you.

⌒

You cannot hate that which God loves so deeply: *you*.

⌒

The gospel is always good news: nothing can separate you
from the love of God in Christ Jesus—nothing! Not your
resentments, not your confusion, not your anger—nothing!

⌒

God always uses us in one another's lives to point always to
him so that more and more he can have more of us so that we
can have more of him.

⌒

We all need to hear over and over and over again the good
news, which is the gospel—that God loves us.

⌒

I believe that the Father would have us ask the Holy Spirit to
make us aware—with little niggles—of those things which
draw us near and those things which tend to separate us from
knowing the love of Jesus.

⌒

The world will tell us that we are unlovable and that we certainly don't merit love and we definitely fall short in all areas and, "How can we think that we are objects of the love of the almighty, powerful creator, sustainer of the universe?" The gospel is good news: God loves us.

~

Just be who you are with God, knowing how much he loves you and that it really is okay to be just you.

~

Have you ever noticed how often the scriptures say, "Do not be afraid"? Of course, those scriptures are there because God knows we are fearful people. We do fear all kinds of things. His reassuring "I am here, I am he, I will be with you" are God's words of love speaking into our fear.

~

Tired, mad, discouraged—there isn't anything that would separate you from God's love. So again, dear one, turn to the one who loves you more than you could possibly know.

~

The Lord Jesus, our creator, redeemer, and friend, actually knows about all our complexities and, I am absolutely certain, does not want us to live in fear. It is okay to make mistakes, it is okay to not do everything perfectly, but it is not okay to allow the enemy to paralyze us with fear. Remember: God delights in you and loves to set you free to use every gift and ability that he has given you through the working of his gracious Spirit.

~

The only place vulnerability is comfortable is in God's loving presence or in the presence of those who we know love us without judging.

2

Invited to Grace
Living Free of Condemnation

I long to become more loving, more fruitful, so much more like Jesus than I am. I want to be like the Psalm 1 tree planted by streams of water: rooted in love and reaching out to others. But I fail, and when I do so, I become frustrated with myself. I am prone to succumb to the temptation to gaze at who I am not, rather than looking at Jesus and who and how he is toward me.

"Express this to Jesus," my spiritual director says after I express my frustration toward myself. "Wait for his response to you. What do you sense he is inviting you to? What might he be saying to you? Who does he long to be to you in this place?" No matter what I bring to Jesus, he is neither surprised nor disgusted by my unfinished state. I peel my eyes off me, look at Christ, and find him to be full of mercy.

Condemnation is like a hammer. It is heavy and used to pound something. When I fall short, I can pound the truth of my own inadequacy into my being repeatedly. Jesus does not deny what I have done wrongly or have failed to do. He sees it all but has no "with-damnation" toward me. Jesus bids me to *reckon with* rather than *run from* his freely given love and overflowing grace.

Often I have done something I know is self-sabotaging, something life-draining rather than life-sustaining, and the last thing I want is for God to see me in my defeated, mangled state. "Invite Jesus into that place to be with you there, and sit with him in your place of weakness," my director suggests. "When you get that defeating thought, look for the Lord Jesus there with you."

So, I crawl to Jesus. If I haven't strength to crawl, I ask him to meet me right where I am, just as I am. There we sit and talk and cry. There he holds me, when I let him, often after I have pounded his chest a bit about how much I wish he would change my circumstances. As I receive Jesus's kind, uncondemning presence, I am able to lay the hammer down. The heavy tool I use on myself and others to pound in the reality of ugly imperfection has no place with Christ. Jesus literally took the condemning hammer's impact for me on the cross. There is no need for it to be used on myself or others.

My husband and I often backpack on sections of the John Muir Trail. On one such hike, we discovered an old sledgehammer leaning against a tree twenty-two miles from the trailhead, far from civilization. It sported a rusted head with an aged wooden handle. It looked like it had rested there a long time. We wondered how it got there and what its story is. Someone carried it far then laid it down. I imagine it will still be there years from now. Who would want to bear the weight of it? Without the hammer, the journey is much lighter. With the hammer, it is unbearable.

Here are some words from Aunt Barb inviting me to grace:

The Lord knows our weakness and does not require of
us more than we can be or do at any given moment.

⁓

God is not in the business of condemning but is always
in the business of loving and healing.

⁓

Our tendency is always to evaluate where we are, and we often
pessimistically think that life will somehow "taper off" rather
than become more and more abundant.

⁓

The Lord Jesus always comes to us with words of forgiveness and never words of condemnation.

⌒

Maybe not so much "ought" and "trying harder" as moment by moment surrendering to Christ's presence and grace. Obviously we don't get it right all the time, but our gracious Lord is always present to pick us up, dust us off, and set us on our feet.

⌒

Yes, letting go of our own expectations, our disappointments, and our frustrations over not being able to change ourselves and others, of not being God :-). Yes, the Lord God wants us to be free of all that, and that freedom comes as we immerse ourselves more and more in the reality of his love. And as you know, being free allows others to be free as well.

⌒

Spontaneous evil or accusatory or judgmental thoughts are always from the enemy. They have no part with you, and you can by God's grace dismiss them. Sometimes the trick is to ask the Lord to alert you to them before they take roost and make themselves at home.

⌒

Remember that God is never the accuser. He is always the one who comes as our advocate.

⌒

Remember that the Lord always knows and is always walking through things with you, even in the midst of your failures and self-disappointments. He is far more compassionate than we give him credit for.

⌒

Our own efforts to do better, be better, and think better are exhausting.

Do not beat yourself up. God is not doing so and does not want you to do this either. He knows about your tiredness and will give you rest.

Jesus does see our frustrations, but note that he is not frustrated or surprised. He does know and does care and wants you to let go of your frustration with yourself. Jesus holds on to us and longs for us to let go of ourselves and cling to him.

We do get frustrated at our lack of perfection. Fortunately our heavenly Father knows what he has to work with and is long-suffering, kind, and patient, always gently moving us in directions which lead to healing and wholeness.

We simultaneously have three channels running in our heads: one which tells us there is absolutely no good in us, nor could there ever be; another telling us we are God's gifts to the world and nothing could be better; and the third is the Holy Spirit channel, which always speaks of truth, that we are beloved children of God with strengths and weaknesses.

We often won't admit it, but our view of God includes someone who somehow wants us to be better than we are and, if we don't live up to that, there will be negative consequences. This of course is the devil's lie and keeps us from being the recipients of God's good gifts, which he longs to give in abundance.

Don't be harder on yourself than God is.

God does not ever want us to be trapped by bitterness, anger, or resentment, no matter what the cause.

~

I never feel that I get it absolutely right, but God always gets it right. It is really important to remember that it is all about what God is doing. Our only responsibility is to "show up."

~

Our emptiness is the opportunity for the Lord to fill us with his glory. If we are full of ourselves, there is no place for him. So in some crazy sense, your feelings of emptiness can also be your offering to God to fill you up to overflowing.

3

Invited to Forgiveness

Embracing and Extending Mercy

F orgiveness. Jesus is all about it. Is not the intent of Christ's sacrifice on the cross to forgive the world of its sin, to forgive me of my sin, enabling us to live and love freely without the burden of shame and guilt, without an impossibly weighty debt owed?

I am often not all about forgiveness. I forget to ask for it, and I forget to offer it. I often don't want to ask for or offer forgiveness; I don't want to need mercy! I can be quite at home settling into resentment and bitterness toward myself and others. This familiar place is a place out of which Christ calls me.

"Come to me" is Jesus's invitation, even—and perhaps especially—as I live unforgiven and unforgiving. My spiritual director will often ask me to spend time with Jesus to confess my sin of commission or omission. "Have you asked for forgiveness?" she will say. "Well, no, because I really don't want Christ to see me like this," is often my response. I allow my shortcomings to become a barrier between Jesus and me. I am so frustrated with myself that somehow I don't want to approach God, fearing, I suppose, he will confirm all the awful ways I feel about myself and declare me a hopeless case.

After I do ask forgiveness, my spiritual director will suggest I spend time with Jesus in that place of forgiveness, lingering with him there. This becomes a time to not just know in my head the fact I am forgiven but to experience Christ's full-of-mercy heart toward me. So I sit. So I wait. With Jesus. He sees my sorrow (or lack thereof). He does not go away. He stays! He hears my longing to be different, how I wish I had not done what I did, the desire to amend my ways. It is as though Christ pulls my hands from where they are, covering my face in shame, and lifts my head, which has been heavy and low with the weight of my guilt. This time of sitting in forgiveness becomes a time to realize (or to put "real eyes" on) his forgiving state and my forgiven state, a time to let forgiveness seep from my head to my heart. When I allow Jesus access to me, I find he is always toward me and forming my heart a little more into the shape of his.

As I have received forgiveness, so must I give forgiveness. Forgiveness is "for getting" and "for giving." I must "get" it before I can "give" it. I wish it were more natural for me to just let mercy flow to others, but sometimes I still dig my feet in, resisting the extension of forgiveness to another.

Soon after realizing my need to forgive someone, I become aware of my incapability to do so in my own strength. My first step on the journey of forgiveness is to pray that God would forgive the offending party. After all, he is way better at forgiving than I. Then I sit with God in my unforgiving place and must wrestle the situation out with him. Of course God forgives, and of course I ought to forgive. But I am utterly helpless to make myself do what I must. Therefore I become utterly dependent on God to help me do what God has said is essential for me to do. Gradually I find myself truly wanting God's blessing on someone who in the past has wounded or offended me and find that forgiveness is occurring in me toward another.

Yes, a million times, yes, forgiveness is a process, one which keeps me leaning into God for help. "Ask God for the grace to forgive," my director often reminds me. This short prayer, "Grant me the grace to forgive," has become my traveling partner on the path of forgiveness. When the memory of heartache or having been wronged by another interrupts my thoughts, seemingly from nowhere, again I pray, "Grant me the grace to forgive." I can tell the process is complete when I find myself truly longing for God's best for the person who has offended me.

Freely forgiveness is granted to me; freely must I grant it to others. It is from a place of being forgiven that I experience freedom to love without the burden of what I owe or think I am owed. Forgiveness is a beautiful, ugly, difficult, awkward, necessary, freeing thing.

When I write to my spiritual director, I sometimes do not want to share what is really going on, how I am truly doing. There is so much I have not done, so much I am not. There are things I have said and done, causing grief and shame. There are cracks in me I would rather not expose. She is like a safe harbor, though, and soon I find myself revealing various layers of me. She is never surprised or repulsed by what I tell her. The love with which she receives me, I know, is the love of Jesus in her as she welcomes me and prayerfully listens, seeing and hearing me with the eyes and ears of my Savior.

Besides receiving the precious gift of her forgiving heart toward me as I reveal whatever seems to me a shameful thing I have done or have neglected to do, she urges me to express to God myself just as I am (the "real" me hanging out with the "real" God, she always says).

Here are some words from Aunt Barb inviting me to forgiveness:

It is virtually impossible for the love of God to flow through relationships based on anything but forgiveness.

∽

The enemy of our souls will lead us down three paths when it comes to sin:

Denial

Guilt

Try harder

Any of them will do to derail us from God's presence. The gospel in light of our sins leads us to truth, forgiveness, and rest.

∽

There is no shame or guilt, sin of omission or commission, fear, or failure that has not been nailed to the cross.

⁓

I think we must decide that we will forgive others and choose to receive the gift of being able to forgive. But it seems also that without the transformation of our Lord, it is impossible. It is somehow a gift the Lord gives when we are ready to receive it. And somehow it seems to be a gift that needs to be received and received and received. We don't always "get it" the first time around.

⁓

Sin is sin. And the Lord is the one who gently shows us our faults, not so we can feel bad, but so we can be forgiven and set free.

⁓

Forgiveness is particularly important, as it is one of the primary things which Satan uses to try to separate us from our heavenly Father. The problem is that so often we think forgiveness is something we have to do, and more often than not, it is a gift from God we have to receive.

⁓

Of course, when the Lord reveals that which is sin, it needs to be confessed and the penitent forgiven and restored. Keeping short accounts with God is always good.

⁓

Think about David. No one fell harder. But he received God's forgiveness and kept on keeping on. The Lord Jesus is described as the "Root of David" (Rev 5:5).

⁓

Forgiveness is that which works in and through us as we face the truth of the incident, whatever it is. We decide by God's grace to forgive, we act in ways that bless and indicate forgiveness, and then we find that forgiveness has actually occurred, that God has indeed done it, transformed us from within, and allowed his forgiveness to flow in and through us.

∽

Forgiveness is incredibly freeing. It enables us to be in any given situation the person Jesus would have us be rather than being controlled by our thoughts toward the one we have not been able to forgive.

∽

We are always to be about building up and in no sense tearing down. It is amazing how deceptive our tongues can be. Praise be to God, who not only points out our sin but forgives and empowers us to overcome.

∽

There is never shame with Jesus. The Lord Jesus never condemns us. He loves us, comforts us, sustains us, and builds us up. If it is sin, then it is to be confessed and will be forgiven. If it is weakness, then he will provide the strength.

∽

It is a good place to be—resting in the forgiving, restoring, healing presence of Jesus.

∽

It's important to remember forgiveness does not involve denial. We are to acknowledge the reality of the wrong that has been done, to pour out our hearts to the Lord, to decide to forgive and ask him to help, to act day by day as though we have forgiven. And at some point, we will know that we are freely forgiving even as we have been freely forgiven.

∽

The Lord is very specific about sin. It is not to be fretted about, mulled over, or the object of intense remorse. It is there, pointed out by the Holy Spirit, to be acknowledged, confessed, forgiven, and then lost in the ocean of God's forgiving love.

4

Invited to Dependence

Acknowledging my Neediness

Quite often as I explore with my spiritual director what is going on in me, something becomes apparent: I need to ask God for help. On the heels of this realization is this fact: I desperately do not want to ask for help, wishing I didn't need God as much as I do. Something in me, seemingly logical, says, as I mature in my spiritual life, I will become more capable in myself and less needy of God's intervention. I wish I could love God, myself, and others in my own strength. I wish I could forgive at will, be self-motivated, have only thoughts that are hope-filled, and possess the merciful, gracious, servant-heart of Jesus.

When I was twenty and my father was fifty, I remember him saying that Christ is made manifest in our weakness. I argued with him, saying God would surely use my goodness and all I did correctly to glorify himself, not my weaknesses and inadequacies. At that point I thought that, because God loved me enough to sacrifice Jesus on the cross, I in turn would, of my own volition, love him back, showing that love by serving others. Because of all Christ did for me, I would live for him.

This plan sounds good, and at the time even seemed possible, but it omits my need for relationship: the journey of relating with Christ Jesus through his Spirit living in me, breathing into me, molding me to be more and more like him, beckoning me to keep in step with him. I can only love because Christ first loves me. I must remain dependent on that love as a branch depends on a vine to even exist, let alone bear fruit. Scripture says, "Therefore, as you received Christ Jesus, so walk in him" (Col 2:6). How did I receive him? By grace, through faith, relying only on Christ Jesus and not on my own goodness. That is, then, how I am to walk in him, in reliance, trusting in Christ's goodness.

I am still surprised by my neediness, by who and how I am not—until I look again upon Christ and his offering to be the one who meets my every need. Jesus is not surprised by my weakness, but as I yield to him, surrendering to him, he delights to be my strength.

Here are some words from Aunt Barb inviting me to dependence:

> Hope centered on our Lord Jesus is the only kind of hope
> that will sustain us in the long run.

∼

> Can't you see how the Father is rejoicing over a child who
> wants only to please him? And of course what is pleasing
> to God is for us to find in him everything we need.

∼

> To know that it is really all about what God is doing in and
> through you is huge. There is great freedom that comes from
> just allowing God to do his thing in and through you in the
> way he knows is best.

∼

> Childlike expectancy and dependency are really at the root of
> our relationship with the Father.

∼

> Sometimes we make it so hard, but all that God really requires
> of us is to acknowledge his utter dependability and our utter
> dependence.

∼

Oh, how we fight our utter dependency on the utterly dependable God. How crazy is that?

∿

I think it is all about recognizing what is going on and then moment by moment surrendering our weakness, fear, sin, or failure to Jesus, allowing him to change what needs to be changed.

∿

Being needy of God is really a good thing.

∿

Life is always too much when we take on the management of our lives. Yes, we are to be good stewards but only in the power, direction, and strength that God supplies.

∿

Steps are steps, and steps made while holding hands with Jesus are steps in the right direction.

∿

When the thoughts come into your head of beating yourself up about needing God's help, open it all up to his presence. Use these thoughts as a trigger to invite him in and see what happens. My guess is that God will smile and say, "I know you are needy. You need to be needy of me, and that is a good thing."

∿

The one thing our heavenly Father asks of us is to know that we are utterly dependent and he is utterly dependable.

∿

One aspect of busyness syndrome is that you rehearse what is on your calendar over and over again and think ahead of time, "Oh, I can never get that done!" Again we need to surrender the future to Jesus as well as the past.

∿

Sometimes we try so hard to get everything just right and at the end of the day it's all wrong from our perspective. So we come back again and again, convinced of our neediness and relying on God's all sufficiency.

~

Saints through the ages identify with the words in the hymn, "I need Thee every hour, every hour I need Thee." Our neediness is all we have to offer God, and our neediness is all he wants to work with.

~

It really is all about what God is doing. He invites us to participate with him (how good this is) but not to manipulate, control, determine, or be responsible for the outcomes.

5

Invited to Entrust
Allowing God to Work in Others

My six-year-old daughter strolled through the mall, one hand holding mine, the other swinging a bag containing three brand-new dresses. We made a quick trip to the restroom then continued our shopping adventure, both of us gleeful about having found such pretty clothes for her. Suddenly we realized the clothes bag was no longer with us, and we dashed back to the restroom to retrieve our purchases. The cleaning lady was sympathetic when we asked her about the bag and took down our phone number in case the merchandise showed up, but it was clear the dresses were gone for good.

I couldn't sort out my thoughts at all and didn't know whether to make this a teaching moment for my daughter or even what the lesson would be. I was partly angry with myself for allowing her to hold the bag and partly angry with her for leaving it in the bathroom. I was tempted to react from my disappointment. I felt sorry for her because she was grieved by the loss, and I felt sorry for me, having just watched $60 go down the toilet! God led me to be with her in her sadness and to entrust her, myself, and the situation to him, seeking what it was he wanted us to know. This was difficult, but I let go and allowed space for God's Spirit to lead and teach.

Hours later we took an evening walk around the block, just Karis and I. As we walked hand in hand, she looked up at me and said, "Mommy, God taught me something really important today."

"What's that?" I asked.

"Clothes don't make you special," she said—a lesson more profound than I could have taught and precisely what God wanted to show her that day.

Such has been my journey of learning to entrust others to God, who is the only one able to change hearts and minds. I need to seek God's heart and wisdom before darting ahead with my natural I-can-fix-this-thing response. I sometimes notice something in another person's life, quickly followed my temptation to repair, to teach, to control, to steer, without consulting God about whether he wants me to say anything or not.

Slowly, I am learning to allow space for God, taking time to ask God to carry others on his big shoulders and speak as only he can into their lives. There are things I want my grown children to know, things I want my husband to know, my friends and other loved ones to know, yet God keeps calling me to be first about me and him, to allow his love to be poured into my life then poured out through my life.

My husband, Brent, often reads magazines about the universe. I used to walk by his reading spot in the mornings and inwardly be disappointed to find he was not reading his Bible. "What a shame!" I would think to myself. In women's Bible studies, as we learn truths about God through scripture, almost all present, including me, have at one time or another said, "I wish my husband would learn this!" There is a longing to teach others what we are learning, to pull them along, but we must consider that God himself may be teaching others in ways unique to them. Perhaps God is meeting that person in a way different from how he meets us. Perhaps God is God over them as well! Perhaps God's longing for them to be close to him is even stronger than our longing that they be close to him! And perhaps only God can bring this about.

As I have sought to see my husband through the eyes of Jesus, asking Jesus to give me his view of my husband, to soften my heart to mercy, I have been freed to better love and accept Brent, while he is freed to respond to God or resist God rather than to respond to or resist my efforts. Now I see my husband has a fascination with his personal creator God, as he stands in awe of the universe.

When I catch him reading the Bible today, my heart doesn't leap as if to say, "Oh, hooray, my husband has finally arrived!" because my happiness does not depend on how I perceive he is developing spiritually. I trust God to meet him in ways unique to Brent.

As my spiritual director and I converse about my concern and care for my loved ones, she repeatedly directs me back to God, urging me to ask for the eyes and heart of Jesus toward others, to entrust them to him, and to ask him where he wants me to come alongside him in loving into the life of another.

Here are some words from Aunt Barb inviting me to entrust others to God:

> One of the hardest things to do is relinquish someone and their spiritual growth to the Lord God, especially someone we care so deeply about.

> ◌

> I always try to remember that the only person I can actually actively participate with God in transformation is me. When I am impatient with others' slowness to change, the Lord often reminds me of his longsuffering with me and my own slow transformation.

> ◌

> Sometimes we think we have to fix things, when it is really only our heavenly Father who can mend hearts and situations. So, proclaim the gospel, the love of Jesus, that unconditional, enormous, personal love.

> ◌

> There is a subtle trap here that I'm sure you're aware of: We don't need to *try* to be role models (we always fail), but to offer our failures, successes, and ourselves to others in love so that they can see Jesus at work.

> ◌

Parenting is so much about grace—grace on our part to let
our children be free to respond to God and his grace to guide,
protect, and grow them.

~

Ask for the eyes of Jesus and his compassionate heart.

~

It's interesting how letting Jesus in on the conversation helps
us to focus on the real needs of others and somehow lessen
the negative effects their behavior has on us.

~

Allowing others space to heal and encouraging them to be
whatever God has called them to be is always good.

~

It is often overwhelming to listen to people's stories, and
because we are compassionate people, we identify with them
and want so much for good to come. It is therefore all the
more important to intentionally give them to Jesus and not
carry their burdens ourselves. They are too heavy.

~

Think of the many persons Jesus encountered who were ill in
a variety of ways. Somehow he managed to love them without
assuming weaknesses or failures on his own part in dealing
with them. Let Jesus's love flow in and through you.

~

You must remember that people who seek to hurt others more
often than not hate themselves so much that it's unbearable. To
them, for whatever reason, making others hurt helps in a very
sick kind of way. It's important that you're able to somehow
separate the "sick" person from the one God created that
person to be. Ask the Lord to allow you to love and somehow
protect you from the assaults of the enemy.

~

Pray the Lord would give you grace to love others and treat them with deep respect despite any response or lack of response you might get. It is hard!

⁓

It's so difficult to see someone we love floundering and without hope. It takes a great deal of the Lord's grace and wisdom so that you can extend love without being manipulated.

⁓

As we pay attention, we see more and more of God's hand at work in our own lives and in the lives of others. He is all about weaving us, each one, into the larger story of his kingdom. How good to be a part of that!

⁓

Oh, how I sometimes wish that I could wave my magic wand and effect changes in other people. I always remind myself of how long it takes God to effect changes in me when I am terribly impatient with the lack of transformation in others.

⁓

We really are members of one another. Sometimes I would like and really love to think that I can make it on my own without any help, thank you very much. But God has put us in families and communities as his gift to us and as his gift to others of us.

⁓

Loving someone enough to desire the best for them is what God does for us daily. How good this is, and of course it brings joy.

⁓

Confronting without caring can be terribly damaging, but so too can caring without confronting. Ask the Lord Jesus to guide you along this path. He somehow managed to confront people and at the same time make them so aware of his love for them that they actually embraced the truth about themselves (for example, Zacchaeus). Make us more like you, Lord Jesus!

~

As we become more and more what God desires us to be, we free those around us because we are no longer pressuring them, expecting them, or even subtly urging them to change. We are free to trust that God will do his thing as we lovingly walk with him.

~

Continue to love others with all the love that Jesus pours into you. Give them the space they need. Be patient with them, even as God is patient with you. And see what he does.

~

You can only help your loved ones by being free yourself to be all that God has called you to be, free from having to respond to that person's moods, free from having to gauge all your actions out of fear of that person's response, free to extend grace to them despite their response or lack of response. Your freedom will allow them to be free, if they will.

~

It seems as though we always need to learn over and over again to allow God to be free to work in our own lives and free to work in the lives of those whom we love.

~

We actually don't know what God is doing in other people's lives (unless they tell us). Sometimes we are right in our guesses, and of course sometimes not. We so much need God to give us faith for our own lives, and sometimes it is even harder to receive that gift of faith for others.

~

The Lord delights to work in and through us to bless others and will give the wisdom required. Remember that you need only to point them to Jesus to help them understand something of his deep, abiding love, and he will do the rest.

~

Lifting your children up to the Lord in some sense is really free-ing them to respond to what God wants in their lives and freeing them from having to either acquiesce to or rebel against you.

~

You've hit upon something that is always very hard to figure: Am I being callous and uncaring, or am I allowing God to work? Somehow the Lord manages to sort it out for us if we listen.

~

Discernment is a gift to be used of God to express his love, compassion, and healing for those around us. The enemy often tries to spoil the gift by immediately turning it into "judgment," and we often yield to this. He also accuses us of being judg-mental, when in fact the Lord is just showing us that which he wants us to know so that we can be better instruments in his hands for showing compassion and love.

~

Overcoming this situation with grace (one-way love) is perhaps God's call for you. This is only possible because you are the recipient of God's grace, his one-way love toward you. "Freely you have received, freely give" (Matt. 10:8b).

~

Loving people who ought to love you back and don't is so very difficult. It's not really about you. It is about their broken-ness, and only the Lord God can bring about the healing and wholeness that is needed for a healthy relationship.

~

When I think of myself and what God has to work with and see that he actually can bring that about, I am encouraged that he can work in and through others as broken and mixed up as I. Our God is a God of patience.

⁓

Take a compassionate look at your loved ones. They are who they are because of their backgrounds, their upbringings, and their circumstances. Your responsibility, insofar as God enables you, is to provide that safe place for them to grow.

⁓

Our task is often to provide spaces of grace for others even as God gives us those spaces for ourselves.

⁓

Sometimes just seeing people through the understanding eyes of Jesus enables us to make a response that is healthy for us and helpful for them. We need to ask for special grace to love and care when we see people "the way they really are."

⁓

Ask the Lord what is best for that person, what is his heart's desire for them. Ask him how you might pray for that person. Ask the Lord if there's any way you could hasten the answer to these prayers. And ask him if there is anything in you that would hinder these prayers from being answered.

⁓

We all desire that "good soil" in which we can grow. Providing that "good soil" for others is often difficult, even when we want to do so.

⁓

Sometimes when we discern something which we know is not of the Lord, our tendency is to try and fix that person or situation. My guess is that most of the time discernment is given so that we might pray and unleash the Holy Spirit to do his transforming work.

⁓

Keep seeing your loved ones through the compassionate eyes of Jesus, always asking to see them with his love.

⁓

Patience and trust are both God's gifts, and, when we exercise them, we tend to bless all those around us.

∿

Compassion calls us to love, care, and support in whatever way we can, but we are not responsible for the outcome. It really is God at work in and through us—not our work for him.

∿

What do you think the Lord is saying to you in all this? Are there things you need to pay attention to or actually do something to help? Are there things the Lord would have you let go of? How would the Lord have you love your loved one? Because this is obviously in the middle of your heart, it's important to listen.

∿

Ask the Lord Jesus to reveal his heart so it might be yours.

∿

It is so good to sort of "sit back" and see what God does in people's lives as they are exposed to means of actually experiencing his presence and love.

∿

We are conduits of Christ's love, and we can rely upon Christ for the results of extending that love.

∿

I can only imagine the sorrow that we cause the Lord Jesus when we fail to love the ones whom he has given us to love. So continue to walk in love, and see him work.

6

Invited to Express

Going to God with Everything

I can sit across a table from friend and, with ease, express to her my frustrations, failures, hopes, dreams, gratitude, and fears. I can share all the moments that make up my life. I can, with my head on my pillow at night, sigh out grievances, review my day, share funny moments and thoughts with my husband. And in spiritual direction sessions, I pull the curtain back on my heart, revealing the light and dark residing within me in the safe space provided by my prayerful director. In all the wisdom she has shared with me, of all the good ideas she has for exploring my relationship with God, one of the most powerful and ultimately transforming ideas has been this instruction: "Tell God what you just told me."

Now, doesn't this seem an obvious course of action to take? Of course it seems so. But I resist going to God. I hold back expressing to God how I feel. Besides, I reason, doesn't he already know anyway? And honestly, when I do express myself to God, I sometimes feel I am only pretending big God really wants to hear from little me.

If my child stubs his toe, I can see his pain. He doesn't need to act as though he feels nothing. Neither does he have to stay far from me or play brave. He can sob in my arms, and I provide tender comfort and needed care. I can ache for him and be present with him in his turmoil.

My dad sat next to my hospital bed while I recovered from a spinal fusion at the age of 13. I moaned and cried in pain while he sat beside me, enveloping my hand in his, saying, "I wish it were me hurting instead of you, Diana." (He is the only person who ever put that extra syllable in my name.) His with-me, empathetic presence brought comfort. As I revisit this scene, I realize my dad *wanted* to be there for me. When my parents, my mother-in-law, and siblings waited at the hospital for my children to be born, they *longed* to be present with me to share my joy. These are true reflections of God's desire to be in relationship with me. Yes, I long for God, but God also longs for me.

Eventually daring to trust that God does care, I, small as I am, do go to God, big as he is. I tell God what I have just expressed to my spiritual director. I speak it. I write it. I wait. It feels like a huge faith stretch to think it matters to God that I express it at all. But there I learn to sense not only what God is wanting me to know, but also who he longs to be to me. I get a glimpse of God's heart—toward me, toward others, toward the situation I am in. I experience the merciful heart of God toward me and am changed. Being at the altar of God just as I am, with my cries, complaints, and utterances, alters me. I become a recipient of perfect love and mercy.

And guess what else I find? Big God really, really does long to be with little me. Yes, all-knowing God already knew what I was feeling, and, yes, he is super glad I felt free to share it all with him. I think I love (yet often resist) that with-me part of God best of all.

Here are some words from Aunt Barb inviting me to go God with everything:

Although most of us have a deep longing for God, we run away. This running away takes on a lot of different forms, but it is good to recognize it for what it is. If we keep really busy, we don't have to face the truth about ourselves and our lives.

∼

Our God knows the up times as well as the down times, and of course he is always present. Just tell God always where you are, how you feel, and your longings to be with him. He will listen, care, and always attend you. When he seems not to be present, turn to the scriptures and read assuring words about his character.

～

Recognize the frustration. Take it to Jesus. Allow him to open your eyes to see the situation through his eyes.

～

I never cease to wonder that God really desires and enjoys our company and friendship. Jesus calls us his friends, and so we are. So, in some sense, we bless God as he blesses us. Even as I write that, it's a bit too much to fathom.

～

God, of course, is real. And the more we bring the "real" us to him, the more we will know his reality and lovingkindness.

～

It is always good to let the real you hang out with the real God.

～

Your longing for God stems from his deep longing for you. We do love him because he first loved us. These deep longings are his gift that he wants you more and more to unwrap.

～

Try to see the Lord Jesus sharing your misery, and begin, if only so little, to be aware of his deep awareness of your grief, and know too that he is grieved.

～

We are weak, sinful, often unable to control our own emotions and reactions. It is important to know this so we might allow the Lord Jesus in his mercy and grace to strengthen, forgive, and grant to us his perception of what's going on around us.

～

It is far better to offer up our helpless, inadequate cries, which are the real us, than to try to formulate prayers we think might be acceptable.

∼

It never ceases to amaze me that, when I take my eyes off of the problem before me or off of myself and look to Jesus, I see the problem (and myself) in such an entirely different way. That always astounds me.

∼

Receive what God is doing with much thanks. Bring questions like, "Why the struggle?" to him.

∼

How might you approach this situation differently if you and Jesus approached it together?

∼

We always need to murmur to the right person in the right place (on our knees).

∼

Allow Jesus to just be present with you, no matter what you are thinking. Remember, he knows it anyway. You might as well just lay it out, because he loves you!

∼

I think the Lord gives us "niggles" when we need to respond to him and let go—those times when we begin to feel tense and feel the need to control an uncontrollable situation.

∼

All of this the Lord Jesus knows, so tell him about it. Tell him about your helplessness, your judgmental attitude. And just like David, ask him, "Create in me a clean heart, and renew a right spirit within me" (Ps. 51:10). It is really all we can do and all we really should do when we come to the end of ourselves.

~

One of my favorite sayings these days is, "Don't fight, invite."
The Lord Jesus does not want us to be alone in a battle, so in
the face of difficult situations, we need to invite the Lord Jesus
into them. Somehow that changes everything.

~

When you are angry, invite the Lord Jesus in. Don't try to fight
it. When you are feeling you must make a difference, don't
fight the feeling. Invite the Lord Jesus in to enable the two of
you to sort it out together.

~

I know it isn't easy, but ask the Lord for an attitude adjustment,
moving from entitlement (i.e., everyone should care about
this) to an attitude of gratitude (I care, and I'm able to do
something about it).

~

God never did give an answer to Job as to the "why" of all
of his troubles. But somehow in God's presence, when he
revealed himself to Job, it was enough.

~

More and more we want to operate and co-operate with the
Spirit's working in our lives.

~

Whenever these thoughts arise, use them as a stop sign to halt
immediately. Then invite the Lord Jesus into your thought
processes. Even at the utterance of the name of Jesus, the
enemy flees. Our heads often go into tailspins that lead us to
do things we would never do if we were thinking with Jesus.
So, don't necessarily fight the thoughts, but invite Jesus to
share them with you, and see what he does.

~

If we allow those anxious moments to be triggers to shift us into God's presence, we find ourselves less and less focused on ourselves and more and more focused on the deep, abiding love God has for us.

∼

The "ick" can only have the power that we give it, and of course it has no power in the presence of Jesus. So, as we use those feelings of "ick" to turn us toward him, the "ick" flees. It's somewhat amusing that we both know what we are talking about when we use the word "ick."

∼

In what you have shared, the Lord is already speaking deeply into your heart. See if you can find those places.

∼

When our eyes are on ourselves, we see, for the most part, all the things about ourselves we do not like. When we look to Jesus, asking to see things through his eyes, all those imperfections, fears, and anxieties somehow are no longer important and we begin to see what he is doing in and through us and can thus rejoice.

∼

Always it's hard to examine our own motives. The only thing we can do is bring that which we know of ourselves to God—mixed motives, manipulative thoughts, laziness or perceived laziness, etc.—and then ask him to purify, sort out, and make right, enabling us to move forward with confidence in his grace.

∼

Psalm 55 always makes me laugh, but this is where we are: "Evening and morning and at noon, I utter my complaint and moan, and he hears my voice" (Ps 55:17).

∼

Turn each situation into a prayer. Ask the Lord to show you
what the real issue is in each case, and then ask him to help
you see it and you through his eyes of compassion and love.
Then pray as the Lord leads you to pray.

⌒

I was reminded the other day that the secret of Brother
Lawrence was his saying, "Good morning, God," every day,
actually saying "hello" to God, no matter what time of day
or whatever the circumstance. He just had the habit of
acknowledging God's presence.

⌒

Dear one, you must always remember that the Lord Jesus
knows your longings, your desires to "get things right" and perhaps is saying, "Chill, my child. I am so happy that you want to
be with me—not as much as I want to be with you, but a little
longing opens the floodgates of my gifting love and presence."

⌒

Jesus is always about inviting us. "Come" is his operative word.

⌒

Inviting, not fighting. I do believe the Lord Jesus wants us just
to invite him into all circumstances of life, not necessarily
trying to fix ourselves in the midst of the situation, not trying
to fix the other person, not fighting for control of either
ourselves or the other person, but just inviting him in and
allowing him to make all the difference.

⌒

Pour out your heart before the Lord. Tell him the desires of
your heart. Allow him to orchestrate the outcomes.

⌒

I was just thinking about Hannah, the mother of Samuel,
before Samuel's birth and the abuse she suffered. She could

have denied her pain. She could have acknowledged it then buried it. But she chose by God's grace to pour out her heart before God and found his healing and restoration. So, fleeing to God is always the best option.

～

Fortunately, the Lord God does know how we feel and why we feel the way we do and takes that upon himself even when we don't quite know how to "present" it to him in prayer.

～

It is always important that we look to God for our "well dones" and "pats on the back" and then be free to receive whatever comes from those whom we least expected to respond or in ways we least expected them to respond.

～

Only the Lord Jesus can deal with resentment and all the other stuff that wells up within us. And of course, he does want to free us. He actually delights in doing so.

～

Acknowledge the truth of where you are. Pour out your heart before him (Psalm 62:8). Let the real you hang out with the real God. Then allow God to do the inner cleanup work that needs to be done.

～

Your confused and weary heart is where it needs to be—in the loving arms of Jesus. "I am my beloved's, and his desire is for me" (Song of Solomon 7:10).

～

I don't think you could be in a better place, going to God just as you are. He really doesn't want or demand anything else.

7

Invited to Discern

Separating Truth from Lies

M y soul has a friend, one who is for me. He longs to lead me and to be with me. My soul also has an enemy, one who is against me. He longs to throw me off course and desires to keep me from being with my true love. Jesus is the author of truth and is himself truth. Satan is the author of lies. In lies he lives, moves, and has his being!

The enemy's deceit is cleverly woven with truth in subtle ways, and sometimes I don't recognize his schemes to keep me from letting Christ meet me wherever I am, however I am.

"Surely you don't want Jesus to see you like this. He's really getting tired of you not getting your act together." The truth is, no, I don't really want Jesus to see me "like this" much of the time. How I wish I could present a more glowing version of myself to God!

Jesus is all about wanting me to be *with* him. Satan is all about wanting me to be, or at least believe that I am, *without* Jesus. Jesus beckons me to *rest* in his love. Satan desires I be *restless* and doubt I am loved. My soul's friend *forgives* and *washes* me when I have messed up. My soul's enemy *condemns* me with a pointed finger, taking delight in drawing attention to my dirty stains.

"Diane is a thirteen-year-old female with severe deformity of the spine," the doctor's report read. I can still see it in my mind's eye right there in the first paragraph, the typewriter font, the off-white paper used to document the doctor's findings about my scoliosis. I purposefully blurred my eyes and read no further. Severe deformity, severely deformed. A skilled surgeon, a seven-hour surgery, a steel rod, and nine months in a body cast served to correct the curvature and stop progression of the disease. I overcame. I became a drill team leader. I was on my high school's dance team. And today I backpack. At my best, I know I am a whole, wonder-filled person who happens to have a crooked spine. At my worst, all that is not right about me threatens to define me and tell me who I am.

There is defamation that occurs on trails close to the trail-heads, where people don't have to take much effort to get to. Litter is strewn about, and graffiti clings to once-beautiful boulders. It is jarring to come across something of beauty that has been mangled so. But go a mile or two in, and the damage becomes less and less, until you find it quite surprising to see even a small amount of trash on the trail. Hikers who venture deeper in display affinity and respect for nature. Like the defamers near the trailhead, the enemy attempts to malign the surface, spray-painting hateful lies on God's creation—me. But God is deeper in me than those surface lies. God cherishes and enjoys my beauty and writes his truth in me, while Satan sprays messages of hate, intended to destroy me.

Often I don't realize what is going on with the enemy's involvement. I find myself believing lies about myself, others, and God. Again I get caught in envy, resentment, and hopelessness, certain I will never be who I was made to be. My director, as she listens, can see what is going on. She reminds me about the enemy of my soul and points me to the friend of my soul. This one who is "for me" speaks life-giving truth into me, labeling me as his beloved, and when I listen to his voice and let him write words of truth in me, I see how ridiculous are the lies of the enemy.

Here are some words from Aunt Barb inviting me to separate truth from lies:

> Self-condemnation really is an attack of the evil one, under-mining the affirmation and love which the Lord Jesus has for us. It is always good in these situations to return to truth: Jesus loves me, this I know, for the Bible tells me so.

∼

It is always good to return to truth in the face of a lot of stuff that sounds like it could be true, half-truths, outright lies, all of which are the enemy's tools used to unglue us.

~

It is often difficult to hear the voice of the Lord Jesus above the clanging, demanding voices both from within and without. When these thoughts come up, it is always good to look to Jesus so that he might show you how ridiculous they are and give you the ability to laugh in the face of the enemy's attacks. Let Jesus lead you from lies to truth.

~

In the crazy world of the enemy of our souls, he would always replace attentiveness and a simple, healthy relationship with God with a tangled, messy involvement in our own weakness and frailty.

~

The enemy's voice is an accusatory one. Having said that, it's not a bad idea to take that "doubting you" before the Lord so that once again he can reassure you of the truth of his grace at work.

~

Lay before the Lord

Truth: where you are right now

Truth: enemy attacks the Lord points out

Truth: Ask God to point out places where you were acting or reacting out of your own woundedness and fear. Confess these things, and ask for the Lord's insight and help.

~

It's amazing how Satan can take a very good thing—your sensing tiredness and needing rest, which are really God's things—and turn it into condemnation! Sometimes we just need to listen to our bodies and, when they say, "I am tired," say, "Oh, yes. I will rest you."

∽

Our God never wants us to flee from truth. He always wants us to view that truth (however ugly) while we are safely enfolded in his arms and free to see truth through his redeeming eyes.

∽

We always think we should be better than we are. The enemy makes us angry and guilty and frustrated. The Lord Jesus speaks peace, forgiveness, and hope.

∽

You can always be sure that the voice of condemnation comes from the enemy, and you do not have to listen to it. Indeed, you should not.

∽

I do believe it's really important to acknowledge truth with a small "t" so that the Truth can set us free. Healing comes when we recognize we need to be healed and actually seek the one who is the healer.

∽

The Lord Jesus can and does help us recognize when we're in a good place (consolation) and when we're in a bad place (desolation). He draws us to himself when we are in that bad place. The enemy never gives up, but of course our heavenly Father doesn't either and is always the victor.

∽

Paying attention to those "little niggles" and ascertaining their message is important. The ones that come from the enemy we should dismiss immediately. They really have nothing to do with us. God's Spirit niggles us with things which bring about healing, wholeness, and blessings for ourselves and for others.

∽

The Lord Jesus knows your need for affirmation and love. The enemy would have you dwell on feelings he generates—loneliness, fear, envy, disconnectedness. The Lord would have you cling to himself, rejecting all that is not of God, confessing what needs to be confessed, and receiving forgiveness.

⌒

Meditate on passages of the love of God. Read, mark, and digest them inwardly, as the prayer book says, and ask the Lord for the strength to say no to the accuser's voice, which whispers lies to you about how it is impossible for anyone, even God, to love such a miserable person as yourself. Sing God's songs of love. There are a multitude of scriptures, hymns, and songs which shout loudly of God's love. And of course, there is always time spent at the foot of the cross to draw you into the realization of God's infinite love.

⌒

It is so very hard to ward off the fiery darts of the enemy when they come at you from someone who is supposed to love you unconditionally.

⌒

I think often Satan would have us spend a lot of time analyzing how we are, how we got to where we are, and commiserating about both. All the Lord Jesus wants of us is to come to him, tell him what we think is going on, and allow him to sort it out—and to sort us out.

⌒

You are the beautiful human being God has created you to be and not the distorted image the enemy projects.

⌒

The enemy of our souls would always try to entrap us in our past, convincing us that nothing can be done about the wounds and scars that have developed over the years.

The Lord Jesus always speaks liberating, healing words and brings about wholeness.

⁓

The enemy of our souls knows just how to suck us into ugliness. But God is the God of redemption. I don't know quite how God does it, but he does redeem even the worst of situations. That redemption is a process, and only God can orchestrate that process as we allow him access into all our hurt, anger, disappointment, and despair.

⁓

The enemy likes to work overtime on our imaginations. Keep taking thoughts captive to Jesus.

8

Invited to Healing
Bringing Wounds to Jesus

"Poor girl," the hairdresser said. "I've never seen such thin hair!" She called over every stylist in the salon to show them the thinnest hair she had ever seen. The huddled women moaned signs of pity for 10-year-old me. The news of my featherlight hair was not new to me. "Poor Diane," my parents would say to each other far back as I can remember. "What happened to her hair? It's so thin! Maybe it was the medications taken to keep us from losing her during the pregnancy." This is one of the I'm-not-okay messages sent to and received by me in childhood. We all have some: arrows that didn't bounce off the surface, lodging themselves in a place they did not belong, in the who-we-really-are part of our hearts. While I have read and even chosen to believe Jesus rejoices over me with singing and I am the apple of his eye, his joy, and his delight, something way down inside me sometimes still doesn't believe it and cries for it to be true.

I sit in a church pew watching my daughter's high school choir perform. I love Christmas, I enjoy music, and I adore my daughter. But what's getting my attention? Forty-nine of the fifty girls on the stage have long hair, and in my heart I'm saying, "No fair! Oh, Jesus, have we not dealt with this? I long to be grateful for how you made me. I desire to see me as you do and to enjoy the beauty of others without envy. And really, would the world have begun spinning the wrong direction if you had managed to dole out some more hair to me when you made me?"

I call on Jesus to be with me in this place, and he is there. He brings to mind a scene from long ago, wherein my two-year-old nephew Tyler was sitting on my lap facing me, gently, slowly stroking his little fingers through my hair as if it were the most special thing he'd ever seen or touched. And in that memory, Jesus hints to me that Tyler's adoration of me is reflective of how Jesus sees me. The jealousy falls away, and together we take in the beautiful sounds of the singing choir and rejoice in the beauty and talent of the people God created.

Jesus has made me whole. I am broken still. I don't exactly get this, and I surely don't like it. Here I am again, jealous me; here I am again, invisible me; here I am again, my spinal deformity defining me. My chin has been lifted by the hand of Jesus but sometimes hangs in shame yet again. Much healing has been accomplished within me, and much healing is yet to be accomplished within me!

I have been encouraged by my spiritual director to read scriptures wherein Jesus is healing a person, to put myself into the scene, to picture myself touching Jesus, to put an image to Jesus touching me. There, Jesus and I converse. There, we weep. There, I pound the chest of Christ and express how hard it is to be me. There, again his love quiets me, and together we sift through the pain-inducing event. Like a child with a splinter running to her parent, I show him the hurting places in need of a healer.

I share this one strand of something that has brought me pain, but it is something also that has made me run to my healer, who has saved and is saving, who has healed and is still healing, who has shown his heart of love to me and will do so again and again.

As my spiritual director and I converse, God brings many areas to the surface, revealing places still needing his touch. She reminds me that God allows these wounds to show themselves so he can bring about further healing and show me more of himself. I am seeing these times when wounds resurface as a chance to know more of God and to let God know more of me. I share this poem I wrote expressing what it is like to have Jesus meet me in my wounded places—yet again.

Layers

There it is again
That area I thought was healed
The ordeal I thought was done
The fight I thought was won
"Another layer," they say
Another layer of healing
Brought to the surface
Not so much the revisiting
of an old wound
As a brand-new visit
Of a brand-new aspect
Of the same old wound
It feels like, here we are again
But here I am anew
Looking at another layer of me
Looking at another layer of You
I want to scream in frustration
At myself
For not getting over my issues
But Your Presence finally
quiets me
Until at last we sit with what is
Sifting through it all
Together

My ineptitude, Your affirmation
My ingratitude, Your generosity
My stubbornness, Your patience
My unforgiveness, Your mercy
My illness, Your hand of healing
My fierce anger,
Your infinite kindness
My ceaseless "whys,"
Your ceaseless Presence
My exhaustion,
Your breath reviving
Urging me to surrender
To rest on your Big Love Ocean
To know You
To know me
To know You in me
And me in You
Again
And yet again
Within these layers
Of me
Discovering layers
Of You.

Diane Mann, 2013

47

Here are some words from Aunt Barb inviting me to let Jesus heal my wounds:

Healing comes in surprising ways. Getting "stuff" out into the "Son Light" is the surest means of healing.

∿

For reasons only known to him, God more often than not does not intervene in the natural consequences of living in a fallen, broken world, where accidents, diseases, and deliberate acts of evil impact our daily lives. So, what to do? We pray for healing and trust that, despite our physical limitations, God is perfectly able to carry out his will in and through us.

∿

Recognition of an attitude is the first step of surrender to the Lord Jesus.

∿

It's difficult to be free to do and be what you believe the Lord wants you to do and be when there is this nagging opposition. The Lord knows this as well, so when it rears its ugly head again and again, return to the Lord and say, "Here it is again, Lord. Please give me the freedom to hear your voice above the voice of discouragement, and be free to work in me the way that will please you and bless those around me."

∿

Enjoy the freedom that God gives you. And don't accuse yourself for that which is not perfect in either your doing or your thinking.

∿

The Lord knows the damaged inner part of us and understands its origin and its relentless, ongoing presence. Sing songs of praise for how far he has brought you and cries of dependence for him to transform from within.

∼

Jesus is the one who brings about inner healing, allowing things to surface so he can touch and make them whole. Contemplative prayer is often the time when God does a lot of inner work.

∼

Another thing which is true with all of our emotional needs is this:

We need to look to the Lord Jesus to meet them in whatever way he chooses. So often those we think should be the ones are not the ones God chooses to use. If we are open to these surprises, we can be thankful, but if we are expecting individuals to do this or that, we often end up grumbling and complaining because they can never do enough.

∼

Even though it is painful, remember the Lord Jesus knows your memories and the effects they have on you. He desires to free you from their crippling effects. He is the one who brings about healing and wholeness and, in doing so, sets you free.

∼

It is so important to know that the God who created us really knew what he was doing! God knows what he intends for us and is busily working in our lives to bring about his intention that we become all he has created us to be. We are being re-created in Jesus, him being the one who really knows how to do so.

∼

Allow the Lord to forgive you, and give thanks for one more opportunity to allow him to heal you of those hurts that you have buried. They pop up in order for him to heal, not to make you feel guilty or ashamed.

∼

The Lord God knows it all, and I suspect he weeps over my sin as well as the sin of all those who name his name. We do get really icky when we don't have the Lord's point of view. I think it is the grace of the Holy Spirit in our lives saying, "No, you don't have to go there. You don't really want to think that way. That is not of me, and you don't have to own it."

∼

God never shows us things that are askew in our lives to torture us. He shows them so that he, in his mercy and grace, can transform us, not by our trying harder but by our yielding to his presence and his love.

∼

God alone is healer of our wounds, and as we honestly expose them to his love, he does all things necessary to bring about healing.

∼

It is my experience that those deep sobs often come from God himself, allowing stuff to be released that we either do not know or should not know—things that need to be released and healed. It is okay to let that happen. Often God uses our tears for our healing.

∼

Tears are Jesus's gift of healing to you. They need not be tears of regret, anger, sadness, or hatred. They can be redemptive in the sense of allowing God to wash away that which has hindered you from receiving all the love which he can pour into your life, and by his so doing, you can pour out toward others.

∼

If the Lord brings things to the surface, you know that it is for healing and not for ill.

∼

We would very much like to be able to instantaneously change our inner thoughts, feelings, and attitudes and find that we cannot.

Only the Lord Jesus can heal from the inside out, and of course he does this step by step.

$\backsim$

I wish that we were impervious to hurts of the past and, of course, those of the present as well. I don't know at all what God is teaching us when those pangs occur, but I do know that he does come and both comforts and heals when we turn to him in those moments.

$\backsim$

This is all bringing tears to my eyes. Healing of deep, profound wounds is a long process. Let yourself cry and grieve, and receive the comfort that only the Lord Jesus can give.

$\backsim$

Sometimes God brings insight into our past so that it might be healed and made whole.

$\backsim$

Sometimes the things which we are most sensitive about in others are things which we really don't like about ourselves. Haven't you seen characteristics in your children that you don't like and you recognize them in yourself? Fortunately, when the Lord shows us things, he shows them within the circle of his love and care for us. That love, of course, is also the transforming power of change.

$\backsim$

To know that we are wounded and bleeding and to cry out for help is really all that God wants from us. You are doing that, and it is all good. God is not disappointed in you—to the contrary, he rejoices over you with singing.

∼

Healing often takes time, and the Lord is always patient, gentle and kind. His desire is that we be free in him, not having the way we think and act be tied to past painful experiences.

∼

Don't try to tackle everything at once. Just sit with the Lord with the specific objective of allowing him to come and do the healing work that needs to be done.

∼

Obviously the Lord is bringing to the surface the things that he longs to heal. Ask him to specifically show you some particularly hurtful times. Ask him to share the experience with you. Ask the Lord to show you his redemptive purposes, and ask him for the healing of those memories.

∼

I have the sense that the Lord Jesus has come and is coming to comfort you and, if not to make sense out of all the circumstances, at least to let you know that he is present, he understands both the circumstances and you, and continues to enfold you in his love.

∼

Your willingness and ability to see your own weakness and areas where you most need the help of the Lord God is always the beginning of the work of grace in your life.

∼

God is always able to redeem bad situations—not calling them good but somehow working in and through us to transform us and the situation.

∼

Let God bring up what he wants rather than letting the accuser throw you into tailspins about everything that is wrong all at once.

~

No matter how far we step back, God is always before our thoughts, our fears, our anxieties. Remember who you are talking to. Ask him to change what needs to be changed. You can't do it anyway.

9

Invited to Encouragement

Rejoicing with God

"You're doing great, Mom," said my son, calling up to me from the ground on which he stood as I ascended a rock-climbing wall. As he spoke these words, not only did hope infuse my psyche, but physical strength flooded into me, enabling me to complete the climb. My son put courage into me with his words.

My spiritual director has done the same as she has journeyed with me. She has become a valuable historian who reminds me from whence I came, who can say at times, "Yes, the road is long, but look how far you've come!" or, "This is what I see God doing in you, and it is a really good thing." I am rich to have someone with whom I can share both struggles and victories.

Vulnerability in showing my heart by letting another have a glimpse into what is going on inside me in the spiritual direction relationship is necessary and can be difficult. When the person with whom I have shared the burden, having listened prayerfully to the hard experiences, comes alongside me in celebration for all God is doing, joy is inevitable. Sometimes my director and I share what I would describe as balloons-and-confetti time when together we celebrate God's goodness. God invites us to these times of noticing the good he has accomplished in my life and the changes he has wrought in my heart and, with us, rejoices.

Here are some words from Aunt Barb inviting me to rejoice in the good God has brought about:

You are listening, and God is speaking.

∼

Keeping the main thing the main thing is obviously what you are doing—loving Jesus and loving others. Somehow I don't think you can go wrong with that.

∼

I think you have received something better than medicine— you and God working together, making things that used to seem so difficult easy—things that were unthinkable, now doable—freedom to think of yourself in positive terms, thus freeing you to be all that God intends you to be.

∼

Some of the things you shared brought tears to my eyes as they reminded me again of how faithful our God is. Grateful for all he is doing in and through you. Grateful for you.

∼

Our ways are not always his ways, but of course, because we are made in God's image, sometimes they are. Sometimes it is very clear that we are really walking in his ways. More and more that is true of you.

∼

It is so obvious to me that God is at work blessing you, blessing others through you, and transforming you into the likeness of his Son.

∼

I hope you are aware of how amazingly God is at work in your life.

∼

As we sit with each other each month, it is interesting to me that the Lord Jesus invariably reveals to you as we chat back and forth the deep truths of his love.

～

Wow, Diane, to know why you feel the way you do and
then to allow God to rescue you with his raw grace and
raw power—what more can one ask? You are in a good
place, the place where he is. Stay there :)

～

And so we give thanks for his faithfulness. All I can say is, "Wow."
I know it isn't a theological term, but perhaps it should be.

～

Grateful with you for all God is doing—shaping you into
the likeness of the Lord Jesus. Growing pains are natural,
even in the spiritual realm.

～

It seems as though the Lord is giving you new eyes to see
things which are hurtful and untrue and giving you the ability
to not allow them to stick to you.

～

As usual, you and the Lord Jesus have worked through so
much. I'm so grateful for his gracious working in your life. Let
him be his gentle, loving self toward you. Be kind to yourself
even as your heavenly Father is kind.

～

It does indeed seem like spring, rivers of living water
welling up within you.

～

I cannot help but rejoice in all that the Lord is doing in and
through you and in the transformation—both in the physical you and the spiritual you—though they are not actually
separate—that has taken place over the last several years. I am
overwhelmed with gratitude.

～

Jesus loves you, my dear, and is so obviously at work.

∼

Yea! It sounds as though you are operating out of the
self that God created you to be.

∼

As usual, beloved child of God, you are listening and hearing
and responding to his love for you, and it is beautiful!

∼

You have so clearly captured the joy as well as the adventure of
God's working in your life. Being able to see clearly and rejoice
are both gifts of God.

∼

Again you are with Jesus, which is a very good place to be.

∼

The kind of exasperation you are experiencing must delight
the heart of God—so much longing for him, so much loving,
so much wanting to be what he desires you to be.

∼

You are where you need to be: turning to the Lord Jesus in
every circumstance, not leaning on your own understanding, trusting in his grace, allowing him to open your eyes to
see all he is doing in your life.

∼

As usual, it is God who is so amazingly at work in your life,
and I am grateful with you for all the insights and freedoms
that you are walking in these days.

∼

It is very apparent to me that you are coming to know yourself
in ways that are healthy and good and also to see God as he
really is. You are able to see your faults without condemnation,

and you are seeing God as the compassionate, loving Savior that he is. This is what I call "letting the real you hang out with the real God." It really is good stuff.

~

A new source of freedom for you: deliverance from fear of forgetting, fear of not being appreciated, fear of somehow never being what God intends. Hooray for being free to be, day by day, what the Lord Jesus wants to work out in you and through you!

~

All blessings to you, lovely child of God.

10

Invited to Discipline
Entering Spaces of Grace

Hearing the word "discipline" used to make me to cringe. I would step way back from the idea of discipline, thinking there is no way I will ever step up to the plate and *make* myself do what is required of me. My husband used to joke around by saying the only thing I was consistent at was drinking a Diet Coke every day! His assessment was not so far off at the time.

I now view discipline in a way entirely different from how I have seen it in the past. I consider my intentional time with God to be a time and space, an activity or cessation of an activity to which God invites me, a time in which he does what needs to be done. "Come to me" is his invitation. My part is to show up, to present myself to him, and allow him access to all of me.

I have a photograph of myself walking on a high trail which steeply drops off on either side. It has been explained to me that disciplines can be like being on that trail. Off one steep slope is the danger of thinking "God does all the work; I needn't do a thing." Off the other steep slope is the danger of striving to do it all myself. "Christ died for me; now I will—with all my effort—live for him and make myself more how he wants me to be," is the dangerous thought down that side of the trail. But in the middle is the place where I show up and present myself to God, acknowledging I can do nothing on my own but am dependent on him to make me more like Jesus, depending on God to give me desires he wishes me to pursue, granting me the will to do what pleases him.

The ways I intentionally spend time with God, seeking to show up in that space of grace, vary. These times I see as my response to invitations from him. Rather than, "Oh, I have to make myself write in my journal," for example, my journaling time stems from God's initiation, the Spirit of God beckoning, "Hey, Diane, I would love to meet with you in your journal. Let's spend time together there." Do I fail to show up? Yes! Do I show up again? Yes! God shows grace to me and patiently teaches me through my attempts to exercise disciplines. Somehow knowing these times are at God's initiation and are his means to make me more like Jesus (rather than my trying to be more like Jesus on my own) has turned discipline into something desirable, drawing me in rather than making me want to run from it.

During a time of journaling I processed a painful memory from my childhood. In my home in the '60s, long shag carpet covered the living room floor (orange shag carpet, at that!). My mother, like many mothers, routinely raked our carpet. I remember her raking behind me, not wanting my footprints to indent the perfectly raked living room floor. I made an effort to walk more softly, to try to not indent the carpet. I internalized this and other situations from childhood and concluded I was a subtraction, taking away from the environment of wherever I was.

As I prayed and journaled with this memory, God gave me the idea to walk with him on the lawn to see what he thinks of my walking on his carpet! For a couple of months this became a discipline, a way I entered into God's presence, intentional God-and-me-together time. I would walk around the outside edges of the lawn then circle my way in toward the center, the whole time being aware of Christ walking with me, sometimes in silence, sometimes listening for him or talking with him. There we shared sweet times getting to know each other more. Finally, I would sit in the center of the yard and be still awhile. Something true about God planted itself inside me as a result of our times together: the truth that God made this earth for us (and me) to enjoy. I sensed his delight in watching me tread on his "carpet."

Most of the time my intentional time with God includes journaling, asking Jesus to show me the gifts he gave me the day before for which he would like me to give thanks, sitting quietly in God's presence, and savoring portions of scripture. But there are times he calls me to meet him in different ways for a period—singing a song with him, playing my guitar while paying attention to God's watching me learn and his enjoyment of me, learning a hymn on the piano, or interceding in prayer in a more concentrated way than I normally would. There are seasons wherein I focus on certain disciplines more than other seasons.

When I commit to meet with God in new ways, I need to be willing to do something at which I perform poorly. I may not "be good at" a certain discipline, and sometimes I may not show up, failing to meet the commitment I've made. Like a toddler learning to walk, I fumble, and God, a loving parent, is not disgusted with my awkwardness. I find the grace of God in both the failures and the successes of spiritual disciplines. New steps are awkward, and refusing to evaluate my own performance is necessary.

My director has described spiritual disciplines as spaces of grace. I love that description, and I long to RSVP "Yes!" to such invitations to meet with God.

Here are some words from Aunt Barb inviting me to join God in his spaces of grace:

Being still without an agenda is difficult, but it's something that allows you to surrender to the Lord and allows him to heal from within in ways that you may not have thought possible.

⌒

I think our fast-food mentality invades the church as well. Scripture is to be savored, and we are to allow the Holy Spirit to bring forth the fruit thereof.

⌒

Remember the key to centering prayer is just allowing God access to you without your interference. It's all about resting in his presence. You need only bring yourself.

∽

The absolute necessity of gratitude keeps us from *pride* in thinking we can do it all and keeps us from *despair* when we find out from experience that we cannot do it all.

∽

Ask God to help you with making sure there are times for you and him, despite whatever else is going on.

∽

Spiritual disciplines are gifts from God. They are those spaces of grace which God provides so he can be free to do in and through you that which is pleasing to him.

∽

It is important not to try to repeat experiences. We put ourselves in places where the Lord can speak and bless but are not to be disappointed if the next time we spend with him in this way we do not receive the same kind of experience. Our experience of him is really up to him. We show up, and God does the rest.

∽

"Lord, have mercy" is an excellent prayer whenever these hurtful thoughts flood into your head. "Lord," meaning, you, God, are utterly dependable; "have mercy," meaning, I am utterly dependent. It also means God is allowing you to refocus on him as opposed to focusing on yourself.

∽

If we abandon ourselves to loving Jesus instead of the instruments that bring us into his presence (prayer, fasting, study, meditation, worship, contemplative prayer), he is glorified—manifest—and we are who he intends us to be.

∽

Ask the Lord to guide and direct your steps. "Send out your
light and your truth, and let them lead me" (Ps 43:3a).

～

Sometimes I describe disciplines as "spaces of grace" which
God always graces with his presence.

～

A good way to approach a rule of life is to assess what
you are actually doing now—how much time spent with
family and friends, how much time with work, how much
time in recreation and how much time in worship—then
think about those things that would be helpful (after
prayerfully laying them before the Lord Jesus) and begin
slowly building them into your life.

～

Being Christ's disciple is what "discipline" means, and
of course he alone makes that possible.

～

We are all about becoming who God intended us to be, the
unique us becoming like Jesus. Hard to wrap our heads
around this, but that really is God's plan. We all look different
and yet are becoming like the perfect lover of our souls.

～

Centering prayer is one way of offering up our love for
God without any words.

～

The Lord delights in your coming to him and delights in the
things that bring you joy in your times of reading or journaling. The Lord will show you how to order or not order your
life in ways that give his heart joy. He rejoices in your coming!

～

It is impossible to articulate what goes on when we offer ourselves to God in silence. What is he doing? How can I know? Is he doing anything? Well, of course we cannot know, but we often see the fruit of such encounters. We find ourselves more centered, less likely to be judgmental, less likely to be disturbed, and we find ourselves filled with peace. It is clear that God just wants us to be with him, not because of our erudite prayers but because of love—his for us and ours for him.

～

We definitely need that sacred space where meeting God is the primary thing and often the only thing we do in that space.

～

There is a difference between being "drawn" and being "driven." I suspect our heavenly Father knows we tend to "drive" ourselves, and what he really wants is for us to be "drawn" into those spaces of grace which he so amply provides.

～

God works in and through us to establish patterns of grace that bring health and wholeness to our entire beings. Establishing a rule of life, for me, is just a fresh call to look at what I am about, allowing God to reveal that which is really good and needs to be kept in place, that which needs to go, and that which I really need in order to be more fully his. As we intentionally look at things through his eyes, he can structure our lives for his glory.

～

Sometimes it is good to sit in silence and allow God to minister his loving presence to you. You may not be "doing" anything, but he is doing everything that needs to be done.

～

The enemy is always at work. We often need to just cry, "Help!" and see what God does. "Lord, have mercy" is a wonderful prayer all the time. "Lord" acknowledges his sovereignty, and "have mercy" acknowledges where we are.

～

It is never a good time to give up "time with God" but especially not when we are experiencing desolation. Isaiah 30:15 is a wonderful verse: "For thus said the Lord God, the Holy One of Israel, 'In returning and rest you shall be saved; in quietness and trust shall be your strength.'"

～

We can smile because God is not finished with any of us yet. As we more and more by God's grace recognize our own weaknesses, inabilities, stupidities, etc., we can move more and more into the places of grace he has prepared for us.

～

Ask the Lord how he would order your times with him. Ask him to quiet your heart. Ask him what you need to read, what you need to surrender, remembering that the time alone with God is his time to do in and through you that which he chooses.

～

Centering prayer is a bit of a mystery—actually, a lot of a mystery! I do not know how God works, but I do know that somehow he is always at work and is always about the business of transforming us into the likeness of Jesus.

～

We cannot nourish or replenish ourselves. There is a fine line between *doing* and *receiving*. We can place ourselves where we've received refreshment before (spiritual disciplines, spaces of grace), but we are not to look to these for the refreshment. The refreshment comes from God alone. Just because we do the right thing doesn't mean an automatic, push-button response from God. He knows our need and will refresh us in his own way and in his own time.

~

Sometimes it is good to memorize either a portion of scripture, a Psalm or a hymn which is "just there" in your head when you need it. Pick something that is meaningful to you, easily memorized and recalled.

11

Invited to Discover

Finding Jesus in the Ordinary

One of the biggest yet most rewarding leaps of faith I make is to believe, as much as I am able, huge, big, creator-and-sustainer-of-the-universe God wants to be part of my days, my moments, my now. Yet if God is everywhere and is "loving toward all he has made," (Ps 145:13), he is present here, he is present now, and he longs to keep company, yes, with ordinary me in my ordinary activities.

I consider myself seriously task challenged. I love and tend to relationships, but doing physical chores and being aware of my physical surroundings are not my strength. It was suggested by my spiritual director that I invite Jesus into my doings, that in the ordinary I notice him and let him keep me company. Sometimes I talk to Jesus during my time performing a task. Other times I quietly let him be with me. I have even carried a lit candle from task to task in my home as a reminder Jesus is leading me, is with me, and can make any activity a holy time.

Once, I consecrated brownie-making to God, seeking for it to be a him-and-me experience. "Lord, you know how uncoordinated I feel in the kitchen. Ugh, look how carelessly I stir this batter. It's flying everywhere!" Then I continued in silence, with an awareness the Lord was hearing me and watching me. I sensed him there not with condemnation but with kindness, communicating to me, "Yes, I know how klutzy you feel in the kitchen. Let's do this together." He seemed to enjoy watching me stir, witnessing me creating brownies. He saw my heart longing to bless another with a dessert. His eyes were absent of a critical look, a lens through which I saw myself.

God has helped me make decorating decisions, listening while I explore ideas stirring within me, and celebrated with me a job completed. We have shared a sweet ashes-to-beauty talk as I clean out the fireplace. He has helped me decide what to keep and what to give away in our discussions as I declutter my bedroom, listening to me say, "I just can't give this away yet. It means too much to me," as I pull a pair of pajamas out of the give-away bag and stick it back into my drawer.

Yes, God is way out there in the universe holding it all together, hugely beyond my imagination, but he is also right here in me, around me, in each breath, in each step, in each heartbeat. Life is more adventurous and tasks are less burdensome when I live with awareness of extraordinary Jesus with me in my ordinary days.

Here are some words from Aunt Barb inviting me to find Jesus in the ordinary:

> Probably more than you know, the Lord Jesus is walking with you, sharing your thoughts, your fears, and your fondest dreams. Let him in on all those thoughts. Allow him to just be present with you.

～

> Sometimes our space reflects who we are. Sometimes our space determines who we are. God is giving you opportunity to allow your space to reflect who you really are and setting you free from letting your space determine who you are.

～

> How often, if we actually verbalize our thoughts to the Lord Jesus, does he shed his light upon the situation and set us free to do the next thing.

～

God is the God of the little things. Isn't that good to know?

∽

Remember it's really about all of life being surrendered to the
Lord Jesus. Each aspect of life is sacred.

∽

Jesus calls us to be free—in any situation—to do those things
which are pleasing to him, not reacting to the expectations
or acts of others.

∽

Being able to pay attention to what is going on with you and
to pay attention to what God is saying to you through what is
going on are precious gifts. He speaks so often, and often we
do not hear because we are not paying attention either to our
own circumstances and reactions to those or to what God is
saying to us through these circumstances.

∽

Somehow God makes every space a sacred space, a space
where he is not only present but calls us to be present in
that space with him.

∽

Surrender to God's presence and grace moment by moment.

∽

It's hard to grasp that God does not look at us in sections
or compartments of dresser drawers but sees us as whole
individuals, every part of which is his dominion. He is a
seamless flow of grace in our lives, no matter what we are
about—scrubbing floors, properly dressed, attending to
our jobs, holding our grandchildren, or listening atten-
tively to someone. You get the idea.

∽

Allow the Lord to give you joy in the thing you are doing
at the moment. Sometimes it helps to give thanks in the
midst of what you are doing *for* what you are doing. We
are always dependent on God to do anything at all, and it
always helps to see Jesus with you doing things with you
and in you and through you.

⁓

It is so true that even simple things, harmless in and of
themselves, in the light of the Savior's eyes, are those
things which can separate us from the things we really
should be attending to.

⁓

Only the Lord Jesus can renew our spirits, but sometimes it
is helpful after we have actually done something we ahead of
time dreaded doing to say, "Thank you, Lord. I did it!—maybe
not wholeheartedly or as well as it could have been done, but
thank you." Somehow the shift to "Thank you," if only momen-
tarily, lifts our eyes off of ourselves and onto the Savior
—always a good thing.

⁓

Imagine a rather large circle, and on the circle are the various
aspects of your life—friends, work, church, exercise regimen,
relationships with a variety of people, etc. Then there is this inner circle where Jesus dwells. Most of us live our lives on that
outer circle, and because we are good Christians, we check in
with Jesus about most of these things. We are always "checking
in." But I think God wants us to dwell in that inner circle with
Jesus so that our relationship with him affects everything on
that outer circle. Everything radiates from him.

⁓

Make a list in the Lord's presence of what needs to be done.
I do believe, as we surrender our tasks to him and live that

moment-by-moment life that he so longs for us to live, at least some of the stress will be relieved.

～

The Lord Jesus would have us more and more living each moment with him in the various activities of our lives so that more and more we are his, allowing him to manifest himself through us no matter what the circumstance— and of course for ourselves enjoying the peace of his presence in each circumstance.

～

Savor the moment. Each moment is a moment that is ours as a gift. Sometimes we miss the present because we are in "our heads," either remembering what was so good about the past (leeks and onions in Egypt) or daydreaming about or fearing what might be in the future.

～

Sometimes it's hard for us to conceive of Jesus talking about fishing nets or the price of meat in the marketplace, but I'm sure he did. At the same time he was always drawing people into a closer and deeper relationship with himself.

～

You and I would always like to "order" our days. Sometimes, more often than not, "The mind of a man plans his way, but the Lord directs his steps" (Proverbs 16:9). Somehow we have to believe, by God's, grace that no matter what, he is ordering our steps day by day.

～

Remember he is in everything and wants to be in the very center of all you are and all you do.

12

Invited to Rest

Ceasing from Strife

I am not my own. I am God's. God owns me. According to scripture, I am God's masterpiece, his poem, his love letter, his vessel, his servant, his child, his sheep, the apple of his eye, and his very own. It is he at work *in me*, not solely I at work *for him*. A song I spend much time singing is "In the Garden," and I am especially touched when singing the words "And he tells me I am *his own*." Sometimes I sing the words to God, "And you tell me I am your own." I would like to park my life right on that one line of the song. In fact, I sing those words much slower than the rest of the song. On "my own" I can do nothing, Jesus says (Jn 15:5). But when I am living as "his own," much fruit I am promised to bear.

How does this look in real life? I am still finding that out, but I can tell you how it looks today. I am in the mountains in our cozy cabin having an alone day. I have not written anything in this book for almost a year. Finally, I am sitting down to type, but I get distracted (well, truly I become fearful and resist writing). I stand to go reheat my coffee, and my foot catches on the cord to the oil diffuser sitting next to the computer. Water with lemon and lavender oils launches across the room, splashing onto the wall, soaking into the carpet. I untangle my foot from the cord to fetch cleanser and cloths from the kitchen, soak up the mess, and refill the diffuser. I put the lid on the diffuser and tip it over again. It pours out a few more ounces of water, puddling on the table then dripping onto the carpet.

I cry. And I yell out to God, "I can't do this! You see how impossible this project is for me?" I am in misery. I read below what my director has said about resting in God, about letting God accomplish what he longs to accomplish in and through me, and my attention is grabbed by these words: "When you think about all the things you are *not* doing, rest. Picture yourself as the little child in Psalm 131, and rest in the Father's arms. Find a quiet place, and do just that."

So, I rest. I find a spot in the window seat, adjusting positions a few times, pretty certain I am doing even this all wrong. I lie cushioned and curled and sob, unable to picture Jesus or the Father. I try to picture myself in his lap, asking him to hold me. Finally, the pillows around me begin to seem like his arms, the cushion below me, Christ's lap receiving and supporting the weight of me, the weight of my burdens. There I rest on him, wholly dependent. He reminds me this is his work, not mine, and the words of Jesus rise from inside me, "Walk with me and work with me" (Matt 11:28–30, The Message). I put on that perfect-fitting yoke, yield to his leading and sit back down at the computer, not with a ton of faith but a bit more than I previously had—faith that indeed Christ is at work in me.

Here are some words from Aunt Barb inviting me to rest in God:

> You can offer yourself just as you are, but that's about it.
> He, in his mercy, will do the rest.

∽

> We are always in the presence of God, but we do not always acknowledge that. The quiet times are so good because they are obvious times of recognizing his presence.

∽

> Assurance does not always come when we think it should, but somehow we know. The Spirit witnesses with our spirit, and we somehow know, even without great fanfare, that he is at work and it is okay.

∽

Christmas *is* amazing, but not because *we* make it so.

∽

There are times when we just need to be still

and *know* that he

is God

(Ps 46:10).

∽

Your task is only to ask, to rest, and to trust. What would that
look like to you on a day-to-day basis?

∽

You are not alone.

∽

We can actually live lives of "expectancy," not expectations of
ourselves but expecting God to work. And of course he does.

∽

Listening to the Lord,

Hearing his call,

Receiving his grace . . .

What can be better than that?

∽

An understanding of how much it is really about Jesus working in and through you lifts the burdens the enemy puts upon
you of should, would, could have, ought to, etc.

∽

When you think about all the things you are *not* doing, rest.
Picture yourself as the little child in Psalm 131, and rest in the
Father's arms. Find a quiet place, and do just that.

"Surely I have calmed and quieted my soul, like a weaned

child with his mother; like a weaned child is my soul
within me" (Ps 131:2).

⁓

Stop *trying*, and ask the Lord for the grace you need. You
will not be able to muster it up within yourself. Ask for the
grace. Behave as though you received it to the best you are
able, acknowledging all the while that even that behavior
is a grace—and see what God does!

⁓

Maybe you don't have to grasp it all. Just relax, and
experience God's grace.

⁓

To the extent that we see all of life as redeemed is the extent
to which God can and will bless *all* of our lives. Our attitude,
however, is to be this: "It isn't all about me; it's all about you,
Lord, and what you are doing in and through me."

⁓

God doesn't even want you to do it all yourself. It really
is his business to transform you into the likeness of
Jesus. Of course he will do it and has begun by giving
you this heart desire to see it happen.

⁓

The Lord is the one who knows you better than you know
yourself, knows precisely what you are thinking and feeling, and
so obviously has gently spoken to you. Receive, and give thanks.

⁓

How good God is to come to us and speak just the things
we need to hear.

⁓

Sometimes I wonder how we get so muddled that we
think we can do a better job than our heavenly Father.

~

By living in anxiety over the future, we miss what God
is actually doing in the present.

~

The contemplative life is all about dwelling with Jesus and letting him call the shots about everything in our lives. For some
people that may mean they are "doing less," but from God's
point of view I think it means they are now doing what he has
called them to do with his power, grace, love and direction.

~

St. Augustine's motto, so to speak, was, "Love God, and do as
you please." Our primary job is to love God so that he can do
in and through us what he desires to do. We are then not ruled
by what we think we "ought to do" either for others or for him.

~

There is always a fine line which separates just cooperating
with God's Spirit and what he means to do in our lives (we
need to do this) and somehow taking charge and making it
our own project which we then present to God (we really
should not do this, as ultimately it will fail). Self-help in and
of itself is not transforming.

~

I have often shared this feeling of, "Why aren't I doing more?
What in the world is wrong with me? Am I just a slug or a sloth
when it comes to the kingdom of God?" But I'm quite sure that
God is more interested in our "being" than in our "doing."

13

Invited to Become

Being Formed to Look Like Jesus

"I am constantly becoming who I already am in Christ," I often heard my father repeat as I was growing up. Initially this made no sense to me, but I saw him trying to wrap his mind around it as he sometimes paced and pondered aloud through my childhood home.

Romans 8:29 tells us we are *being conformed* to the image of Christ. I used to think the second I received Christ's forgiveness and proclaimed him as my Savior and my Lord, I was already like him. I thought the work was done, the price paid, and I was a new creature. All true! Somehow what also is true is Jesus is still at work in me forming my heart. I am a new creation, and I am becoming a new creation. Once I was blind, and I am learning to see. Once I was lost, and I am still being found.

My children's youth pastor likens receiving salvation and journeying through life without relating with Jesus to someone who gets into Disneyland for free, steps through the turnstile, but stays close to the front entrance. He or she might never venture deeper into the park to experience what it offers, yet still declare to everyone outside the gates how wonderful it is to be inside. I do not want to tell people about a savior whom I am not continuing to know.

I am easily influenced by others' opinions. When I am shopping with a certain friend, I gravitate toward clothing she would like. She has an influence on me. As I am closer and closer with

Jesus and get to know him more, I take on Jesus's eyes and heart. I notice what he notices, my heart gets excited for that which excites him, and I begin to be drawn to those things that he thinks merit my attention.

A becoming-like-Christ analogy God has shown me is to see people as votive candle holders with the light of Jesus inside, the Holy Spirit inhabiting each of us, each holder having been created uniquely. Whatever pattern God used to decorate my candle holder (personality, passions, gifts, traits) is different from others', thus individuals reflect creatively and uniquely aspects of God he wants to show the world through each of us. He is causing to fall away various outside decorations I have applied to myself in attempts to look how I think I should as a Christ follower. I continue to become who he made me to be, one through whom Christ desires to uniquely shine.

The exciting thing is, sometimes I see it happening: the heart in me conforming to be a bit more to be like that of Jesus, the light shining through in a way he intends. When I am not conforming and become discouraged about my slow, sometimes backwards-seeming growth, I experience his mercy and patience. I am learning that to be constantly *becoming like* Jesus, I must constantly *be coming to* Jesus. My director points out to me time and time again that Jesus is in the business of transforming me to be more and more like him, using the all the ingredients of my life to do so. It is both a mystery and an adventure, this constantly becoming who I already am in Christ.

Here are some words from Aunt Barb inviting me to become:

> One of the beauties of the gospel message is that God
> has uniquely created each of us, loves each of us deeply
> and is about the business of redeeming, transforming,
> and shaping each of us to be all he has created us to be.
> This not only frees us but allows us to free others up to
> be who God intends them to be.

~

He is not a vindictive God, nor one who stands aloof from us, waiting for us to pull ourselves out of the mire in order to please him.

∼

Remember you are focusing on the *real* God—not the one that accuses, judges, leaves you bereft (the one that Satan would have you believe in). As you focus on who God is, joy will well up in your heart.

∼

God is infinitely kind to us, but we are not often kind to ourselves.

∼

Always remember that you are a testimony to God's grace, whether you think so or not. Do you fail? Oh, yes, but in your failures you also testify to the gracious, loving God, who picks you up, dusts you off, and stands you on your feet.

∼

It is said of the Lord Jesus that he learned obedience by the things which he suffered. I cannot imagine all of the assaults that the "heavenly being" Jesus would endure in the fallen world. So take heart. The Lord isn't finished with any of us yet.

∼

We are all slow learners. How patiently our heavenly Father leads us step by step, holding us, picking us up, dusting us off, and setting us on our feet again and again and again.

∼

The enemy always wants us to focus on ourselves—how bad, how guilty, how impure our motives are. And all God wants is us, just the way we are.

∼

It really isn't about what we do for God.
It's about who we are to him.

~

God really does delight in you. The gifts, abilities and talents which are yours are gifts from him, enabling you to be all he created you to be, becoming more uniquely you and becoming more and more like Jesus.

~

Being free to be what God wants instead of what you think other people want is always both hard and scary.

~

God is always about redemption—taking our imperfections and bringing about that which is beautiful.

~

I too always want that "zap" which somehow makes all my imperfections disappear and imparts only holiness, righteousness and love. I suspect that the Lord knows we would not know how to act if that were the case. Incremental growth is really God's design, his design that we might walk with him, have fellowship with him, and be his friend, even as he is a friend to us.

~

A lot of what we are to be about is just allowing God to flow through our lives in whatever way he chooses. After all, he did make us the unique creatures that we are, and he alone knows best how to draw out the very best of all of those unique qualities.

~

Little steps are all that is needed. Fortunately, our God knows exactly where we are and does not expect us to leap from where we are to where we think we ought to be. Satan will always use that against us: "By now you should be so much better. Why aren't you?" God says, "Take my hand, and let me lead you step by step. We are doing this together, and I am the one who knows the way. I will not only show it to you but give you the power to walk in it."

◠

The Lord is using all of this to set you free from the many should-haves, could-haves, didn't-dos, etc. which have been so much a part of you. He is helping you to walk in freedom to enjoy the you he has created you to be.

◠

Trust God to develop and grow in you those things which will bring him glory as you become all that he intends.

◠

Each of us is a unique creation of our heavenly Father, and each of us is in that process of allowing God to free us to be all that he created us to be.

◠

The crux of the matter is owning who God created you to be and being, by his grace, able to shed the things that are others' expectations and pressures on you, embracing boundaries set by the Lord Jesus, not necessarily by you just to protect yourself. He is the one who loves you completely and is your protector.

◠

God knows the desires of your heart, and of course those desires are his as well. He delights in those desires.

◠

It would be good to remember that the Lord Jesus knows you better than you know yourself, and I suspect those things which you consider great character faults are things which he lovingly laughs about and is all about using them for his glory. He can do that, you know. Allow those floodgates to open, and by his mercy and grace, shut out the things which tend to imprison.

◠

Jesus sees the beautiful creation he has made when he looks at you. He created you, redeemed you and loves you just the way

you are! Always return to the truth when your head is spinning out of control with thoughts which are not in accordance
with the good news of the gospel. One antidote to this head-
spinning thinking is to give thanks for that which you can do
and are. As you do this, the Lord Jesus will open your eyes to
see more and more of the beauty that is you.

~

Because of the way we were raised, our backgrounds,
and the myriad of circumstances of our lives, there are
all kinds of pressures which often distort or move us
away from that beautiful person God intended us to be
from our creation, using the intelligence, the talents, the
abilities, and the skills that are his gift to us.

~

We are all very different, and we are who we are by God's
loving creation. So, give great thanks for all that you are. God
is not the least bit surprised by anything you come up with
or put off by your being you. Always remember he loves you,
not the person that you are trying to be or the person you
think you ought to be.

~

It is one of the paradoxes of the Christian faith that we are
to love ourselves and die to ourselves. Die daily to that old
self and keep coming to know that true self which God
has given to you.

~

Others have tried to rob you of your beautiful self, and God
has returned it to you in a big box with a big bow, and you are
slowly unwrapping that self, that good gift he has given you.
Now that it's yours, it needs to be his.

~

When we are occupied with the myriad of things with self
at the center, it means we are bowing down and worshiping
the god "Me." I don't know about you, but I'm not very good
at being God. When we are aware of these things going on, it
is good to put Jesus back on the chair of our lives. We often
bump him off and put something else in his place. We can
use these situations as triggers that allow us once again, over
and over, to allow Jesus to be Lord.

~

Again, allow the Lord to let you be just you: the loving mother
he has created you to be, not the perfect mom, not the perfect
Christian, not the perfect example, just who you are. Who you are
is really okay with the Lord, so who else do you have to please?

14

Invited to Serve

Blessing Others

"Blessed to be a blessing" is my paraphrase of something God spoke to the Abraham in Genesis 12:2 and a phrase residing in my mind from my earliest memories. I understand the concepts of loving others because Christ loves me, letting him work through me, being a vessel of his grace and love, and being the attached branch to the vine, who is Jesus, resulting in life-giving fruit being borne. All these things I comprehend, and all these things I desire.

But what does it look like in real life to have Christ do his work through me? How does this really happen? What is my part? What is his part? Like the hymn "Take My Life and Let it Be" says, I long to have Jesus "Take my hands and let them move at the impulse" of his love.

While my father was hospitalized after becoming a quadriplegic, he was unable to feel anything below his face or to move at all, other than to slightly tilt his chin. I would sometimes lay my head on his chest, draping his arm over me to receive a hug from him. Physical therapists taught our family how to bend his limbs to keep his blood circulating and prevent atrophy. Could my father move? Well, yes, technically his limbs could move by our manipulating them. His body could not receive impulses from his brain, however, because of his severed spinal cord.

Often my service to God looks like my dad receiving physical therapy. I am moving at the will of outside forces: my own perceived obligations, others' expectations of me, how I believe Christian service is to look—a kind of outside-in spirituality.

Presently I am typing. Without much thought, an impulse is traveling from my brain to my fingers, and my fingers move. My fingers are moving at the impulse of my brain. Christ is the head, and we are his body, our movements ideally initiated by and stemming from Christ and his love. He is the conductor of the orchestra, the composer of the music. We each have a part and move at the direction of his headship. A vessel of love, an instrument of grace, a branch stemming from him, these and so many other beautiful pictures are becoming beautiful realities in me.

What I must return to in order to avoid serving through my own strength and will is the intimacy of me with Jesus, Jesus with me. Sometimes I feel I am being selfish when I retreat to hang out with Jesus, allowing time and space for Jesus to restore me and love me. But retreat I must. Jesus himself served others then went away to be with his Father, again returning to serve others. Jumping ahead to "do something for God" looks productive, though he is often asking me to wait and to retreat with him awhile.

As I listen to others, I hear them say they want a purpose to their lives, that "one thing" they do well for God. Most of us have various gifts we use at various times.

My ten-year-old son was anxious about what he was going to be when he grew up. He shared his thoughts out loud as I drove him to the store in our van. "Mom, I just don't know what to do. I don't know what I'm going to be when I grow up. I want to be a teacher, I want to be a football player, and I want to be an artist!" He wrestled with his thoughts a few minutes then, with much relief, blurted out, "I know! I can be an art teacher who teaches people to draw footballs!" Problem solved!

As I live in God's presence, he brings to light desires he has planted within me, unique ways he made me to be in this world. As I have explored these desires and the way he has made me, I have concluded the part of Jesus's body I see myself as is the nape of the neck, the area connecting the heart and the head. I love settling in with people, listening to them sense God in their lives, and journeying with them as they allow love and truth to seep from their heads to their hearts. This is how I am bent, what gets my attention, what I want to continue to grow in—ushering others to Jesus, facilitating a space for them to listen for the Spirit of God in their lives.

I cannot finish out my part of this chapter without saying I feel all too often as though I am not serving God if I'm not in an official capacity in ministry. In other words, if it's not advertised in my church bulletin, I feel as though it doesn't count. The things that count in my mind, though deep down I know better, are speaking publicly (would God not be so glorified if I were standing on a huge stage in the center of an arena declaring his goodness?), writing books, singing a song beautifully while others' souls are being stirred, or having a ministry with a website and a logo. God has changed and is changing this flawed thinking in me, but the thoughts still settle themselves in my mind at times.

During my time in spiritual direction, my director noticed in me a strong gift of discernment, along with a deep care for others' spiritual growth. She encouraged me to explore a training program to become a spiritual director myself, and I have done so. This is my offering to other believers and a way I serve Jesus, something for which he designed me.

During day one of my training to be a spiritual director the class was invited to do a bubble-prayer exercise. We were to see our breath as God's spirit and the bubbles as our works, what we "do for God." Each class member shared what he or she noticed.

"There is no such thing as an ugly bubble," someone shared.

"Some last a long time, and some pop very soon," said another.

"When I force the breath, no bubble is formed at all," noted a fellow student.

"I don't control where the bubble goes, but the wind carries it," the sharing continued.

I noticed that my part is to line up with the Spirit of God, allowing him to form something through me and allowing him to be in charge of the results. I have no control over the results of what I offer to God, of what the Spirit breathes through me.

When I am who God has made, and is continually making me to be—one loved by God—moving at the impulse of Christ, I am living authentically with an inside-out service. What I do begins to stem from who I am and who God is still forming me to be. My service becomes an offering back to God of what he gives to me. My offering may be sending a card or a text to a hurting or celebrating friend, meeting someone for coffee to listen to her heart, making chicken enchiladas for a family with a new baby, listening to and praying for my adult children, cheering them and their children on in life, or hosting a quiet day for others to have a spacious time with God. The ways God chooses to love others through me are varied and creative, and he has really good ideas for my service suited to both the needs around me and the gifts given to me.

Sometimes I still get irked at God for not giving me a microphone. When I am envious of another's gifts, I am gazing upon them with my arms crossed, expressing my "No fair!" attitude. Rather, I long to receive my gifts with gladness—unwrapping and sharing the gifts God saw fit to give me. The Lord has shown me there is a lack-of-gratitude issue going on deep inside me when I look with envy upon what he's given another. Often I must return to giving thanks for what God has fittingly and bountifully bestowed on me.

Here are some words from Aunt Barb inviting me to be realize I can be a blessing to others:

Putting the Lord first more often than not results in our giving ourselves to others.

～

Discernment is a funny kind of thing which God gives us, sometimes when we have actually spent time seeking it specifically and sometimes just an intuitive "niggle" that says, "This is the way, walk in it" (Is 30:21).

～

Being sensitive to what God is doing in other people's lives
is a gift—a precious gift.

⌒

Gifts are things which God gives you the freedom to enjoy
and wants you to enjoy. They are gifts and not things that you
must have in order to be whatever you think you ought to be.

⌒

Good things always happen in and through us because of who
God is. God uses us when we are broken, while we are being
mended, and while we at least think we're in good shape.

⌒

We are all, of course, "needy" in different ways, and I think
that's one of the reasons we are called to be a part of the body.
We make up for one another's weaknesses and benefit from
one another's strengths.

⌒

It's always important to acknowledge that we are *not* God. He
is the real tender of the garden. The gifts are his gifts, and he
knows exactly how and when we are to use and develop them.

⌒

Basically, God showers us with so much that is really to be
surrendered to him so that it can be used appropriately in our
own lives and to bless others.

⌒

God gives us treasures and longs for us to recognize them,
value them, and hold on tightly to them and at the same time
hold them with open hands to him.

⌒

The desire to share is really God's gift. However, sometimes we think we have to manufacture something to

share. The Lord just wants us to share what is real and true
in our lives with others.

∽

Often we feel that we're doing nothing, and in some ways we
are. But God is at work in and through us in ways which we
cannot really fathom. Staying close to Jesus is the key. He will
let you know what you are to do and when you are to do it.

∽

Waiting on the Lord is never a cop-out. Over and
over again the psalmists exhort themselves to
"Wait for the Lord" (Ps 24:14a).

∽

It is Jesus who is Lord. And allowing him to be Lord of every
aspect of our lives will indeed bring forth fruit. Ministry as
such will be who we are because that is who Jesus is. Life is
really messy (maybe you have noticed), and it probably is
not a good idea to try to analyze and to force ourselves into
a pattern of our own design.

∽

The Lord has called you into this ministry and will alert you
to all those niggly things that would lead you astray. As you
surrender to him, he will be your guide and stay. The enemy
would love to have us fall back into old patterns, but he knows
nothing of the pattern maker.

∽

It really is all about what God does in and through our feeble
efforts to bless others. In his hands, these feeble efforts are
transformed into abundant gifts of love.

∽

God doesn't always use us in quite the way we think we are
to be used. (Sometimes I think, what are you doing, Lord?)

The bottom line, however, is that he is so gracious to share the work of the kingdom and entrust us with our little part and give us joy in so doing. The Lord has called you. You are saying, "Here am I," and that is really all that is required.

∼

It is about God working in and through us, not what we can do for him but that which we allow him to do through us, which gives joy to his heart.

∼

God has given you that which you can do by his grace. Invite Jesus into both the "doing" and the "entrusting."

∼

You do not need to worry. When God calls you to do something, he always provides everything necessary and will work in and through you to bless others.

∼

Remember you need only to point others to Jesus to help them understand something of his deep, abiding love, and he will do the rest.

∼

Listening to the Lord, hearing his call, receiving his grace —what can be better than that?

∼

Isn't it just kind of fun to watch what God is doing? Yes, we are his instruments, but God is the one who is doing all the real work as we just surrender the gifts he has given us to him.

∼

My guess is that the Lord Jesus is saying to you, "It's all about me. Let me do in and through you that which pleases me, and of course you will be that light I intend you to be."

～

We find that all of this learning is not to be kept to ourselves.
We find others to whom we can be that encouraging word and
faithful testimony to God's love and grace.

～

Caring is a very large part of who you are and the heart
that God has given you.

～

All we have to offer is our utter helplessness and
dependence on God. He takes that "all" and, like with
the loaves and fish, multiplies it in ways that are beyond
our imagining, never mind our engineering.

～

All that I am and all that I have I offer to him. It isn't
as though I have anything else anyway.

15

Invited to Remember

Real-eyes-ing God's Goodness

I would not liken a spiritual director to a trail guide but rather someone who has witnessed my journey, seen where I have been, sat with me when I have lost the trail, and high-fived me at the mountaintops, all the while sharing the joy of God showing me new things.

On hiking trails my husband will point out to me geographically where we have been. "There's where we started our hike. We then came around that mountain, down that canyon, crossed the river, then went over that pass." He always knows where we are and where we have been and points to those locations.

Because my director has journeyed alongside me, she too can remember from whence I came. She urges me to recall the goodness God has shown in the past, recognizing how miraculously he has worked in me, asking me to realize (put "real-eyes" on) his faithfulness and to give thanks. She also reminds me to, right where I am, look for the goodness of God. "Do you see the grace here?" is a question she asks to usher me into recognizing what God is up to presently. She cannot see into the future but offers me a sense of where God is always leading me—toward God, toward love, toward Christ-likeness.

When I thank God for who he is and sift through all he has done for me, I experience confidence that he will not cease to be who and how he is. After I write to my director about what is going on, she asks me to go through what I have written and to give thanks to God for changes he has brought about and to look for blessings I may have missed. This never fails to change my perspective of God and my circumstances. Perhaps part of being led "by still waters" as expressed in Psalm 23 is being reminded to reflect and look again upon what God has done. I see the trees, the mountains, and the sky. I see them again in their reflections on the still water.

It's especially important to me after a stormy chapter in my life to review what went on—what are some remaining questions? What were gifts given during the storm I may not have noticed? What does God want me to know of him through this time of looking again upon a situation? Reliving wonderful moments, such as the wedding ceremonies of my children and my grand-children coming into this world (and into my heart!), allows me to slow down and savor God's goodness yet again.

Here are some words from Aunt Barb inviting me to remember God's goodness:

Remember who is in charge. The Lord does not always answer our prayers in the way we think they ought to be answered.

~

When you are afraid that nothing is happening, take time to remember and give thanks for all that God has done in healing this area of your life.

~

Look at all God did in this situation. Take some time to give him thanks, but also take some time to look at what he is doing in you, naming those things and giving thanks.

~

When good things happen, we can give thanks for what God has enabled us to do. When bad things happen, we can give thanks for another opportunity for us to trust his grace, mercy, and redemption.

⁓

Somehow just recognizing what God has done already
does indeed strengthen and prepare us for the next
challenge to our faith.

⁓

There are times when waiting seems to be what God is
about in our lives. Waiting is not in any sense wasted. God
is at work in our lives in a variety of ways as we wait. It's also
interesting to look back and see what God accomplishes
through our waiting. We often think we are standing still,
and in some sense we are, but God is always at work doing
his thing in our lives. How good that is.

⁓

Sometimes we forget that God does really know all things, is
always moved with compassion, and always acts on our behalf.

⁓

Reminding ourselves of what God has done gives us courage to
have faith when there are bumps in the road we had not expected.

⁓

God has revealed himself in the written word, the
incarnate word, and the witness of the Holy Spirit. What
kind of a crazy God is this who actually cares about us
individual specks in the universe? And yet that is the
message Jesus came to bring.

⁓

Sometimes when we are physically limited, God uses this
to allow us to see and appreciate things which we could
not see or appreciate otherwise.

⁓

The psalmists regularly called to mind what God had
done for them in the past. Rehearsing God's goodness is a

powerful tool to thwart the enemy. The focus is thus on God and not on the enemy, which is always a good thing. The enemy gets too much of our attention.

∽

Spend some time looking at all God is doing here. I think it will encourage your heart.

∽

Do you notice the grace here?

Epilogue

Three years have passed since the idea was planted in me to write this book. My director and I have continued to meet to explore the invitations of God in my life. The years have brought lovely additions to our family, miraculous healing of my hepatitis C through a new medication, and the sudden loss of my spunky, much-loved mother, who didn't return from a seniors' field trip with our church. Her death, my healing, the marriage of our youngest child, and the birth of our third grandson then adoption our fourth grandson occurred within a short period of time.

I share this because the temptation is to divide life into good and bad things—losing my mom, bad; gaining grandchildren, so good—but life is not so tidy. God leads us through joyful celebrations sometimes with hearts hurting over another matter. Likewise, he gives unexpected joy and light in times of heavy grief and darkness.

"Seamlessness" is a word my director uses a lot lately to describe what I'm living out. As I am more and more aware of God's presence with me, I experience less separation between my intentional "time with God" and the rest of my day. Perhaps this is the ceaseless prayer we are told to engage in, this "being with" God, this awareness of God's being with us in each moment, in each breath.

In Christ I am invited to live. In Christ I am invited to move. In Christ I am invited to have my being. May my response increasingly be "Yes" to those gracious invitations.

If I quiet myself, lean in, and listen closely, I sense Jesus saying, "Thank you for coming to my presence!"

In answer to your question, Aunt Barb, yes, I notice the grace here. I notice the grace.

www.ingramcontent.com/pod-product-compliance
Lightning Source LLC
Chambersburg PA
CBHW070503090426
42735CB00012B/2666